FAMILY SPIRIT

The Origins of Five Generations of the Supernatural

LEITREANNA BROWN

First Edition:
First printing

PUBLISHED BY HAUNTED ROAD MEDIA, LLC

www.hauntedroadmedia.com

United States of America

This book is for those who see and hear what goes bump in the night but have nobody to talk to about those experiences. It is for the ones who can sense what is around them even if they cannot see or hear them. This book is for those who believe the ones who speak of the unknown and want to know more. This book is for you.

To my dad who taught me that great things really can happen outside your comfort zone.

To my mom who taught me to embrace whomever and whatever I am because she always has my back.

To my husband who showed me that as long as we have each other we can handle most anything.

To my children who have inspired my mind, my thinking, and my heart.

Acknowledgments

First and foremost, I thank all of those in my life who encouraged me to indulge myself in the world of the supernatural. The truth is people really love ghost stories because we tell them when we are surrounded by family during a holiday. I hope that as you read our family's escapades, you will picture in your mind how closely our family worked together and how as a family we dove into mysterious thrills while we enjoyed every moment. I am grateful to my Grandmother, Virginia Scott for showing me how to be tough during difficult times, to trust myself even when others doubt themselves, and to embrace that we are different and unique which is not a bad thing!

Thank you, Jess Elliot, for helping me realize that I could be the spokesperson for my family and our paranormal experiences. I doubt I could have captured them without your encouragement.

This book would not be possible without the support and encouragement from Mike Ricksecker and Haunted Road Media. Over the years, he has been encouraging, instructive and approachable which fueled my passion for writing and gave me courage to face the task.

LEITREANNA BROWN

Table of Contents

Introduction

My family is a group of paranormal investigators. Each one of us grew up in a different era and has helped make the next generation of investigators better by digging deeper and deeper into our family's spiritual gifts of mediumship. Additionally, we improved our investigative skill adding more analysis and state of the art technology. My great grandmother started investigating and brought in my grandmother and mother. Meanwhile, my father had his own investigations organized and included cryptozoology so when my mother and father met, they had an explosion of cases, tactics, opinions, and egos. Interestingly, when I was born, I turned the apple cart over because it took all of them to teach me. The next book I write will be how my children challenged all of us as it took all of us to raise my children. Apparently, the spiritual gifts grow with time and with nurturing and education. These cases are real and extremely personal to my family as they shaped who we are as individuals and as a family. I hope they touch your heart as much as they have ours.

Chapter 1

Introduce the Family

Do you believe in ghosts? What if you could see, hear, or talk to spirits, would you tell anybody? Would you value your experiences and want to share what you learn? What would people say about you and what you do? What if you were not alone in your talents for the supernatural? People like you would be your "family," right? What if they were your family? The spirit dimension is real for us. We communicate with the supernatural and we are family. Therefore, we are called Family Spirit.

Why we do what we do? Countless people carry a deep secret that they can see or hear spirits. Sometimes, people have had a supernatural experience and need help dealing with their feelings. With nowhere to turn, they bury memories deep in their mind because other people, often skeptics, stomp out and oppress any freedom to discuss these controversial, mysterious topics. Fear of the unknown, apprehension of what people will think, the anxiety of facing mortality, panic of feeling crazy, and the worry of being ridiculed is only a small portion of the many feelings that ghostly victims feel and, over time, these feelings compound and cause damage just like any painful suppressed memory.

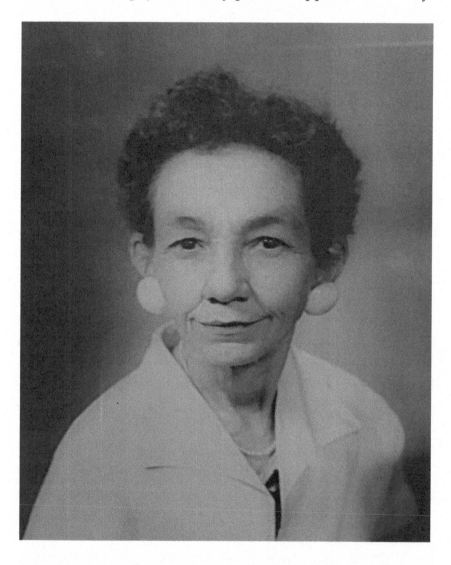

My job as a shaman, paranormal researcher, and spiritualist is to help people and protect my friends, and family so that people can strengthen their abilities and learn more about the spiritual world as knowledge is power. I was lucky to have been raised to question what I see, to embrace all spiritual gifts and to have been taught how to control my reactions as an analyst and a team member. If my husband and I chose another path, our children and grandchildren would have nobody to talk to about their experiences, no one to help with their training, so they would feel isolated and frightened. Embracing our spiritual lifestyle has brought my family closer together. Many places we go, strangers come to us tell their personal paranormal experiences and ask for clarification. Our clairvoyant abilities aid in our spiritual investigations and we see spirits many places we go. Often, we get messages and the spirit world is real to us.

My great grandmother, Guynell Still, (aka Gigi), was a curiously strong, petite lady who was not afraid of confronting large threats with her fire poker as her side arm as discovering the truth about a mystery, and telling the facts about what she discovered. She was of British and German descent and often cooked old family recipes. Since she had polio as a child, she was considered by many doctors to be "crippled" but was a miracle to have lived. Due to her handicap, she had a difficult time giving birth. Out of her three pregnancies, the only child she bore was Virginia. Gigi also struggled with work. Maintaining a job that required her to stand was a struggle for the 4 ft 11-inch lady. Luckily, she was a spitfire and did not give up easily.

During the 1930s and 1940s, my grandmother, Virginia (aka Mama Jenny), often heard about supernatural events. During these hard times, many people lost loved ones to war, went hungry, and were on their own to survive so the turmoil was fertile soil for hauntings. The mother and daughter team took on various ghostly mysteries, praying the entire time, and remaining as fearless in their spirit encounters as they did in life. They were ladies of their era that had a can-do attitude. When my mother, Judy, was born, she fell into step with Gigi and Mama Jenny.

Mom (aka Judy, or Nina), showed amazing signs of spiritual gifts, just like Mama Jenny. Nina possessed the gift of prayer and many people often asked Mama Jenny to add them or their loved ones to Nina's prayer list as they expected results from her prayers. Amazingly, Nina was turning four years old when the prayer requests started to come in. Nina used to go to Mama Jenny's prayer circle meetings. Nina was asked to lead the Christmas Story as Mama Jenny taught her to read early and Nina used her children's bible as reference as she knew the story by heart. When the prayer circle looked at Nina's bible after she delivered her holiday story, she had turned to the correct chapter even though she was a beginner reader. Nina would pick up praying when other ladies passed the duty to other ladies at the circle and her prayers showed maturity and faith. Nina often prayed for the sick and her heartfelt prayers were touching and loving. Since Nina prayed often, the ladies' prayer circle sent Nina the prayer list and started learning that the prayer list was indeed feeling better. When I asked mom about her prayers, she said that she simply prayed without ceasing and that is all anyone can do.

Nina's father, Leon, was an American soldier from the Philippines. He was a descendant of the great purple witch of the Philippine Islands. Did some of mom's abilities come from Grandpa Leon, or did they come from the German and Iroquois ancestry that Mama Jenny carried? Who knows?!

When Judy married Allen Terry (aka dad), a second-generation Cherokee on both sides of his family, a herpetologist, mammologist and crypto researcher, and evangelical singer, the spiritual activity in the family ignited.

Mama Jenny and my dad often did not see eye to eye on spiritual experiences. Dad's membership in the evangelical choir exposed Dad to strict religious teachings and fierce scrutiny from the clergy. In time, dad opened to what we saw, felt, and experienced due to our spiritual gifts. By the time I could talk, dad knew he was in for trouble. I questioned everything, saw spiritual beings, had no fear of talking to strangers even at a young age and about any topic. I challenged his upbringing and fears about what he believed to be true. Although he was traditional in his spiritual beliefs, he was completely open minded about the animal kingdom and nature as he knew elemental and animal spirits existed. He could see animals following their instincts, listening to the great spirit, and following directions, and it spoke to my dad's heart. My father often asked, "Are humans the one animal on the planet that will not listen to their instincts?"

Mom and dad often investigated interesting and mysterious locations just like Gigi and Mama Jenny. Dad often drew the line with allowing me to participate in spiritual encounters because he tried to protect me. Later in life, he saw that I had spiritual abilities and started to embrace the spiritual truths about our entire family.

God smiled on me when he gave me my husband, Matthew Brown. He has his own mystical family from childhood as his family is spiritual. He is well traveled, educated, open minded and without a doubt one of the most honorable human beings I ever met in my life. He is truly a gift from God in my life. Instead of pushing away my spirituality, Matthew was able to embrace it. Matthew was educated and experienced in brutal hauntings since he and his family lived in several homes with supernatural experiences. However, they suffered greatly with an extreme haunting that is beyond most people's comprehension. Matthew stepped into the supernatural realm with Nina, and Mama Jenny and me with grace.

The family moved into the same home together and lived as a tribe where each person carried additional weight to contribute to the entire family. Not long afterwards our children, Mia and Elijah showed incredible, mind blowing spiritual abilities. With the two children added to the fold, there was little wonder why Mama Jenny, Nina, Matthew, and I decided to stick together to raise the little ones. With the children having spiritual encounters as toddlers, the entire family, without training, would have doubted their senses. When the children were old enough to start managing their spiritual abilities, the research for the current generation of Family Spirit began. We decided to open our spiritual family life to the public in hopes that other families would embrace their family's spiritual abilities, learn together, and make a conscious decision to keep a strong family unit. The case studies in these pages are real and we hope that our experiences help all who seek answers.

e will strike at a balloon so the group of
trike at body heat. Sounds exciting, doesn't it?
t to enjoy it!
ed, Mr. Allen will ask everyone to meet at the
ave lunch and show his most recent movies.

*Terry Allen training another kind of animal, the
porpoise, to use in movies and shows.*

Played Jane in Tarzan movie . . .

Dorothy Hart slated to appear in Greenwood Parade Dec. 2

Preliminary plans are in the making to bring celebrity Dorothy Hart to Greenwood to appear in the Wednesday, Dec. 2 Christmas Parade.

Ms. Hart is perhaps best known for her portrayal of Jane in the Lex Barker Tarzan flics, "Tarzan's Savage Fury."

Her career in films began in 1952 when she won the Photoplay Gold Key Award, according to an article by Ralph Roberts in the October edition of "Carolina Film."

She went on to appear in 17 films, opposite such leading men as Randolph Scott, Dennis Morgan, Richard Basehart, and of course, Lex Barker.

Ms. Hart also had numerous television credits from the 1950's and 1960's when she appeared as a panelist on several shows and did dramatic roles opposite Charles Boyer, Burgess Meredith and our now - Chief Executive, Ronald Regan.

Dorothy Hart left Hollywood in 1952 because she felt that her film career was not allowing her to develop her personal potential as a person or in helping others on this planet of ours.

She became the first female entertainer to work on behalf of the United Nations. In 1957 and 1958, Ms. Hart was U.S. Observer at the World Federation (UN meeting in Geneva, Switzerland.

Ms. Hart was on Eleanor Roosevelt's Speakers Committee, which was comprised of people who spoke on the positive aspects of this world-wide body where nations can work out their differences in a peaceful manner instead of resorting to war.

Ms. Hart resides today in Asheville, N.C. and has been doing some commercial work. On Nov. 12-14, she appeared at the Western Film and Memorabilia Festival at the Ramada Inn West in Asheville along with other celebrities such as Sunset Carson, Johnny Crawford, Lash LaRue, and John Russell.

"Ruf" Hammond of Citizens Bus Lines is sponsoring Ms. Hart's appearance and she is being promoted by Terry Allen.

Allen, a wildlife expert, wrestled alligators in several Tarzan movies, as a young man. He is a member of the National Geographic Society and the Smithsonian.

Wildlife expert Terry Allen is shown here with Dorothy Hart, who starred in several films during the 1950's and played Jane to Lex Barker's Tarzan. Allen is promoting the appearance of Ms. Hart in the Greenwood Christmas Parade on Dec. 2. She is being sponsored by Ruf Hammond of Citizens Bus Lines.

Allen & Terry Allen milk the
Diamond Back Rattlesnake
NBC television show.

ALLEN TERRY'S WILDLIFE COMPOUND

On a field trip, Terry shows the students how an eastern diamond rattlesnake looks in the wild and how hard it is to see. He recaptures it before their eyes.

...ike, Mr. Allen will release a rattle snake and let ...can camoflage itself in nature, but don't worry- ...ight before your very eyes! He will also let th... ...group can see how far they ... ...le will strike...

Here's Allen holding a Coyote. He will appear on the Wildlife Show. Another TV Star.

The Allen Terry family. Each holding a pet. Leitreanna, Mrs. Judy Terry and Allen Terry.

Lee Miller, a member of the Allen Terry's Wildlife Compound. Lee feeds, raises, and trains these animals. Here he is feeding a baby Raccoon. The Raccoon is a member of the Show.

Here Allen Terry faces the dangerous Eastern Diamondback Rattlesnake. He faces death many times a year for Scientific purposes.

ALLEN TERRY presents the

ALLEN TERRY'S
WILDLIFE SHOW, Inc.

Lectures on Reptiles and wildlife and nature. Live rare animals, rare Blue Fox, Coyote, Opossum, Ferrets, rare Chickens, Raccoons, Honey Bear, Coati Mundi and Monkeys.

A live TV Show on NBC station WFBC-TV. "The Scene Today" Peggy Denny and Bill Wheeless, both Opera Singers. Allen Terry is holding the dangerous Gila Monster Lizard.

Chapter 2

Ghost Hunting Glossary

Afterlife: Life after death.

Apparition: Any ghost that seems to have a physical presence, whether visual, auditory, tactile, or olfactory.

Clearing: Removing ghostly activity in a specific location.

Cold Spots: Areas of cool air found in haunted locations due to energy being spent by the spirit.

EMF (Electromagnetic Field or Electromagnetic Frequency): A combination of electrical and magnetic fields. EMF fields are generally measured as part of the ghost hunting tactics.

Entity: Often used to describe a spirit or ghosts.

Epicenter: Person or location that a poltergeist or haunting tends to focus on. Paranormal phenomena usually increase when the epicenter is present.

EVP (Electronic Voice Phenomena): The act of catching and documenting disembodied voices and sounds on electronic devices.

Ghost: A entity or spirit that visits or lingers in our world after death.

Paranormal Investigators (aka) Ghost Hunter(s): People who investigate hauntings to find explanations for possible paranormal phenomena involved.

Haunting/Haunted: Describes a location where there appears to be paranormal activity. Often includes a combination of cold spots, apparitions, missing objects, and other phenomenon witnessed by several people which leads to the location getting a reputation for this activity.

Manifestation: The tactile, auditory, olfactory, and visual signs of a haunting.

Medium: Someone who communicates with ghosts and the other side.

Orbs: Spheres of luminous light (often whitish or pale colored), usually captured in photographs. Many investigators believe they represent spirits or ghost.

Paranormal: Anything outside the realm and experiences we call normal. Often used to describe ghosts, UFO's and other phenomena that defy traditional scientific explanations.

Percipient: A person involved with or witnessing a paranormal event.

Physical Manipulation: When an object is thought to be moved or physically altered by a ghost or spirit (such as lights flickering and objects moving by an unseen force).

Portal: A dimensional doorway through which spirits arrive and leave a location.

Primary Readings aka Baseline Reading: The initial measurements of temperature, electromagnetic field, wind, and any other source of activity that can be measure that is taken at a haunted location, used for establishing an investigation's direction.

Psychic: Psychics have another sense other than sight, smell, hearing and physically feeling that they obtain information. Psychics receive info from the spirit or minds of others, depending upon the context. Psychics are people who can see things outside physical laws and perception.

Psychokinesis, also called **telekinesis**, in parapsychology, the action of mind on matter, in which items are purportedly **caused** to move or change due to mental concentration upon them.

Séance (aka Contact Ceremony): A grouping of people gathered to contact the spirit of a deceased loved one or other person (usually consisting of a medium, assistants, loved ones of the departed, or other interested individuals). Many séances were exposed as hoaxes in the late eighteenth and early nineteenth centuries.

Spirit: From Latin meaning "that which breathes," it describes the consciousness or soul of an individual. In the ghost hunting context, this refers to the soul of an individual who has passed on and continues to be observed in an area.

Spiritualism: A belief in the spirit world and/or the ability to communicate with spirits of the dead.

Telepathy: The process by which a mind can communicate directly with another without using normal, physical interaction or ordinary sensory perception.

Vortex: A center of focused or concentrated spiritual energy.

LEITREANNA BROWN

Chapter 3

The Man in Blue

One fall, I had my first paranormal experience when I was seven years old. I remember very vividly the events in detail. I came home from my Aunt's home; I went to my room to play. I got my dolls out of the doll airplane and stretched out on the floor to play. I smelled dinner cooking; mom knew love her meatloaf. The meatloaf always had her special sauce on top and that was my favorite part and I often took a biscuit and sopped the sauce after everyone finished with the casserole dish. I smelled the dish cooking, but I did not have an appetite. I looked out the window of my room watching the sun beams come through my red velvet curtains and the sun made my eyes burn so much that it hurt to even blink. I was flooded with hot and cold chills, so I knew I was getting sick. When mom came to call me for dinner, I told her how badly I felt. She felt that I had a high fever and we both decided that it would not be a good idea for me to try to eat dinner. Mom picked me up off the carpet and put me in my canopy bed, knowing I needed to get a good night's sleep. She helped me change into my genie pajamas, gave me some medicine that tasted like oranges so that my fever would go down, and told me we were headed to see the doctor in the morning. The next day, mom took me to our family doctor, he gave me a shot we felt would help me recover quickly. Instead, I got worse. It hurt to stand, and my legs just would not hold me up and mom realized I was having a reaction to the medication I was given. I cried and prayed for what seems like weeks to recover but children are never good patients. I could tell my mom was very worried about me and I heard her talking to Mama Jenny on the phone and they picked up my school assignments for over a week so that meant I had a long way to go before going back to school.

One afternoon, I heard a male voice say, "Are you OK? What can I do to help you feel better?"

I looked around my room but did not see anyone. I did, however, feel warmer and comforted. Let me try to explain the feeling I had when my spirit detected the supernatural being that came to visit me. I knew he could communicate without words because I felt emotions instead of actual words. I saw pink, yellow, and purple prisms of light that swirled in a huge ball. The mass of colors reached the ceiling and mixed with the sunbeams coming through the window and I will never forget the sight. The swirling was not fierce but rather calming like a glittery snow globe that mesmerizes the mind.

I said, "I wish I could see you."

The voice said, "I think that I would scare you if you saw me. What could I look like to keep you from feeling afraid?"

I remembered what my dad, mom and grandmas told me about angels being so brilliant to look at that our human eyes could not tolerate the sight. I wondered if I was talking to an angel! I knew that I would be frightened if I saw a massive spirit that was so brilliant that it challenged my nerves and my mind to take it all in. I decided to find an image that would be funny, welcoming, and kind after all I was a happy go lucky little girl. I did not want to miss the opportunity to see an angel, but I knew that if I were scared then the angel would disappear, and I would miss this incredible moment. I looked around and saw some peanuts in a container on the nightstand and saw the man with a monocle on the can. I heard the male voice laugh and say, "And would you be alright if I looked something like that?"

I told him that I also thought a British accent would be good as I always loved hearing them when I watched British crime and mystery films with my Mama Jenny. I heard him laugh loudly so I felt I was in good standing already with the spirit and surely, I would not be afraid of the image I selected. I turned my head and saw a tall, thin man, in a blue three-piece suit, wearing a monocle.

His smile was sincere, and his eyes seemed to peer completely through to my soul. He was a transparent, milky blue, but I could see the texture of his hair, the laces on his shoes, and the chain on his monocle so he did not look like a shadow or just some figure where maybe eyes were playing tricks on me. What told me more about the spirit than how he looked, was how I felt with the spirit in the room. I felt like I had been looking for him my whole life as his personality felt familiar and loving. When he moved, I could see traces of his spirit slowly following like a candle does when they flicker. He smiled at me and asked if I was frightened. Assured that I was not afraid of him, he sat down on my bed, smiled at me, and touched my hand and I felt like his spirit was pulsing completely through my skin. I felt the glowing energy resonating through my arms and tingling started down my spine. At first, I felt invigorated that I could see the angel, that I was not afraid, but then I slowly, very slowly, I started to feel relaxed and contented as I unknowingly fell into a deep yet healing slumber which was much needed. Fever often causes me to have nightmares. During this illness, I had not gotten a good night's sleep as my dreams often woke me up. I dreamt I was falling down in a dark gaping hole, and another dream I was drowning then the life was being squeezed out of me by an octopus; I awakened myself with blood curdling screaming. My seven-year-old brain could not remember ever being so frightened of being sick so being able to be contented, calm, and sleepy was more than what any doctor could have prescribed to help me.

The next day, I told my mom about the man in blue. With as much curiosity as concern in her eye, she asked me what he looked like, what he said, how I felt and if I thought he would return to see me. Since she and Mama Jenny had seen angels before, she did not scold me or doubt me but rather questioned me to make sure that I was not being fooled by what I thought was a possible angel when in reality it may have been someone more sinister. My mother was born with a childhood heart condition and when she had serious moments of illness, she saw an angel that helped her through the fear and pain. Mama Jenny dealt with severe abandonment as a child along with moments of emotional neglect from various family members, so she often had supernatural encounters that calmed her mind as she realized that there were many other things in life bigger than the problems she endured.

The beautiful moment I experienced with my new spirit friend helped me understand what my mother and grandmother explained to me about their experiences. I longed to see the man in blue again so I could learn more, feel better, and tell my mom and grandma about what I saw so that we could compare information. Most of all, I wanted to see him again and tell him thank you for caring about me and giving me peace.

After I ate lunch and a snack, I got sleepy again. Sometimes when I slept while I was sick, I had sweats and episodes of what some people call night terrors. This time, I took a short nap without incident. When I woke up, I put my stuffed animals in the bed with me, read a book, and talked to Mama Jenny on the telephone. Even though I was getting better, I could not play or go outside because I did not have strength. But after eating dinner, getting a bath, and dressing for bed, the man in blue came to see me. I saw him walking into my room from my bedroom door and with every step, he became clearer into view then sat down on the foot of my bed. Still looking the same as I saw him last, he smiled with the monocle intact.

Was my bedroom door a vortex to another dimension? I had heard of spiritual vortexes as Mama Jenny had one at her home and we experienced it often, but that did not really matter to me right now. What mattered was that my spectral companion was back, and I felt the bed shift as he sat down on the foot of my bed to talk to me.

He reached over and touched my shoulder and asked if I had more strength today than yesterday. I did not notice any other words he was saying as at that point, his mouth was not moving, but I felt his thoughts. He wanted me to know I was loved, I was safe, and I would feel better soon. He helped me realize that what I do, even as a young child, affects everyone around me and I had to be strong and try to do the right thing even when nobody was around. His kindness cuddled my soul. I had so many questions in my mind for the man in blue. Who was he? What was he? Why did he come to me? Why did I feel like I already knew him? But instead of my questions taking over my mind, the love and peace the spirit poured into my heart took over my thoughts. It was at that point I knew the calling of my life.

The next day my grandmother came to see me and asked me to tell her about the man in blue. She asked if she could see him and I told him that I would ask him. She waited and so did my mom, but he did not come see me at that time. We ate dinner, I knew that I often saw him at night so I was ready to go to sleep and see if he would wake me up. I fell asleep waiting and when I woke up, the man in blue was, again, sitting on the foot of my bed. Mama Jenny already left for the evening, she headed home to wait for a call from mom. Mom was nearby and heard me corresponding with someone in my room. While she heard me talking to someone, she stayed just outside the door so she could understand more of what was going on and so she could be close to protect me.

After the specter left, mom came into my room to talk to me. She had Mama Jenny on the phone. She said that she could not hear the man in blue speaking or see him, but she heard a sound like a bumble bee trapped inside a glass jar. Neither mom nor Mama Jenny could deny how I was improving, and they showed great patience with me as I did my best explaining what I saw and felt. Mama Jenny understood I was connecting with a supernatural being that was loving and helpful, just as my mother did when she was sick, so she wanted to see how I was being affected being able to see him and interact. It seemed silly for anyone to worry or question the man in blue since I could feel his goodness, love, and happiness even when he did not speak. Mama Jenny and mom were so happy for me that I had my own experiences. I wrestled with the emotion that other people could not see him and believe I am delirious. My supernatural encounter with a lovely spirit who made me feel better, made me smile, and helped me was so comforting that I was content to keep my secret from other people and enjoy my visits with him. I am so thankful that my mother and grandmother did not think I was having a delirious fit but rather having a real moment with the supernatural. Dad was away on a business trip, when he returned home, he listened carefully to everything that happened. He knew I had been sick. He was not convinced that I experienced a spiritual being because my fever was so high, but he was happy that I was healthy again and that I had a meaningful experience and that I learned a wonderful message. He conveyed to me other stories of people that encountered possible angels. Dad helped me feel comfortable and blessed.

Throughout my life, I have continued to see the man in blue on various occasions but not for long periods of time. He does not always appear to me in the same form. However, his voice is unmistakable as I recognized his voice and the tone of his guidance as he is always reminding me to accept my mission of peace, love and understanding others. I gained a new perspective for the paranormal and it was the beginning of a desire in my heart to learn more of the unknown. Little did I know, the man in blue experiences was the start of a lifetime of the paranormal.

Chapter 4

Mill Village Prelude

I have lived in a southern mill village community most of my life. The early textile industries not only built their factories, but also built entire villages for their employees where the cost of rent for the homes was taken out of their checks. Mill villages often followed a simple house layout, with workers housed in rows of identical single-family houses, or in some cases, duplexes. Supervisors lived in larger homes closer to the mill. Mills usually built churches, schools and even hosted a baseball league. Lots of people on in the mill village were very close since everyone worked with each other and lived close by. Every person in the mill village, watched out for everyone's children. When the mill had an employment contract with an employee, they often had it with the entire family and all family members as child labor laws did not exist at that time. Also, if someone was fired from their job, or the resigned, they also lost the use of the mill village home. Once someone moved into the village, they often stayed for several generations.

Lots of the experiences I will discuss in these pages will take place on the mill villages across the south. Surprisingly, the mill villages have stood the test of time. When all these homes were built, short cuts were not taken but rather built with solid materials and maintained well over the years. Since so many generations have lived in these homes, many are not surprised that these homes have living history dwelling in them. The lady in white is a specter from the mill village community. This is her story.

1930 Mathews Mill

LEITREANNA BROWN

Chapter 5

Ghost Hunting History and Definitions

For as long as people have been spooked by sights and sounds in the night, people have investigated the unknown. If you believe in ghosts, then you are in the approximate 50% of the world that believes spirits survive death and live for eternity with us or in another realm. Millions of people in the world believe in spirits and many cultures in the world support the same belief that the eternal soul exists. Many folklores, old ghost stories, and spirit communication promotes the idea that people want the comfort that their beloved deceased family members are with us, helping us, and are beside us when we need them.

In the late 1800s it was popular for the wealthy ladies to hold seances in their parlors with tea and cakes. Ivy League schools established ghost clubs. Psychic mediums often performed their talents in rich people's homes across America.

In 1970s, TV shows aired series about the unknown and mysteries that were unsolved. Finally, in early 2000s, TV shows came out showing groups of analytical people, using many scientific methods, to search for ghosts. These paranormal TV shows were a huge hit and dozens of other shows sparked off the original ones. From the paranormal shows, thousands of paranormal teams all over the world formed and started using social media to post their findings. All the ghost hunting teams need is some free time, some locations with historic hauntings, some devotion to the field, and some technology.

Glossary of Paranormal Terms

Below is a list of basic terms that are commonly used during paranormal investigations:

Afterlife: Life after death.

Anomaly: Something that cannot be explained.

Apparition: Any ghost that seems to have a physical substance, whether visual, auditory, tactile, or olfactory.

Clearing: Getting rid of ghostly activity in a specific location.

Cold Spots: Areas of cool air found in haunted locations.

EMF (Electromagnetic Field or Electromagnetic Frequency): A combination of electrical and magnetic fields. EMF fields are commonly measured as part of the ghost hunting process.

Entity: Any being, including people and ghosts.

Epicenter: Person or persons that a poltergeist or haunting tends to focus on. Paranormal phenomena usually increases when the epicenter is present.

EVP (Electronic Voice Phenomena): The act of capturing and recording disembodied voices and sounds.

Exorcism: Ridding a person or a location of evil spirits by using religious rites.

Ghost: A sentient entity or spirit that visits or lingers in our world after death.

Ghost Hunters: People who investigate hauntings to find explanations for possible paranormal phenomena involved.

Ghost Lights: Mysterious lights, seen at a distance, usually appearing as blue or yellow spheres, which can appear to blink.

Haunting/Haunted: Describes a location where there appears to be significant paranormal activity. Often includes a combination of cold spots, apparitions, missing objects, and other repeated phenomenon witnessed by several people which leads to the location getting a reputation for this activity.

Manifestation: The tactile, auditory, olfactory, and visual signs of a haunting.

Medium: Someone who communicates with ghosts and the other side.

Orbs: Spheres of translucent light (often whitish or pastel colored), usually appearing in photographs. Many investigators believe they represent spirits or ghost.

Paranormal: Anything outside the realm and experiences we call normal. Often used to describe ghosts, UFO's and other phenomena that defy traditional scientific explanations.

Percipient: A person involved with or observing a paranormal event.

Physical Manipulation: When an object of some sort is thought to be moved or physically altered by a ghost or spirit (such as lights going on and off and objects moving without any human interaction).

PK (Psychokineses): Also known as Telekinesis.

Poltergeist: A spirit who makes noise or plays pranks. Often thought to center around specific individuals (such as teenagers) and perhaps not ghosts at all but rather a form of latent telekinetic ability.

Portal: A doorway through which spirits enter and exit a location.

Possession: When a person, or even inanimate object, is taken over by a spirit or ghost.

Primary Readings: The initial measurements of energy taken at a haunted location, used for establishing an investigation's direction.

Psi: A term for "psychic phenomena."

Psychic: Can relate to the spirit or mind, depending upon the context. Psychics are people who can see things outside physical laws and perception.

Residual Energy or Haunting: When emotionally charged events leave an imprint or energy residue on nearby objects and locations. Residual energy or hauntings will often repeat a specific event from the past over and over again, as if on a loop, such as the same footsteps walking down a hallway.

Revenant: A ghost that only comes back a few times after death.

Séance (aka Contact Ceremony): A gathering of individuals to contact the spirit of a deceased loved one or other person (usually consisting of a medium, assistants, loved ones of the departed, or other interested individuals). Many séances were exposed as hoaxes in the late eighteenth and early nineteenth centuries.

Spirit: From Latin meaning "that which breathes," it describes the consciousness or soul of an individual. In the ghost hunting context, this refers to the soul of an individual who has passed on and continues to be observed in an area.

Spiritualism: A belief in the spirit world and/or the ability to communicate with spirits of the dead.

Telekinesis: The ability to control one's physical environment without using physical manipulation or force (also known as psychokinesis, TK, or PK).

Telepathy: The process by which a mind can communicate directly with another without using normal, physical interaction or ordinary sensory perception.

Vortex: A center of focused or concentrated spiritual energy.

Pictured above is some of our paranormal equipment from 1990s. The photo is from our night vision camera. We set up several stations like the one pictured above featuring a split screen television. These types of monitoring devices are maintained by one of our investigators at the command center (or centers depending on the size of the location) when we use our full equipment and not just handheld equipment.

Chapter 6

Lady in White:
A Mill Village Specter

One of my closest friends in middle school, Stacey, came over to my house to spend the night on a blustery, fall, Friday night. We wanted to watch a TV show that was sure to give us goosebumps, so we were thrilled my parents said we could watch. I love the Halloween weather, the candy, and the costumes. The night wind was blowing, and the sun had set for the night, so Stacey and I went out to the car to get her bag before rain started. The howling gust scared us as we grabbed her bag and ran back very quickly to the house, slamming the door behind us giggling the whole time as most girls do. My parents laughed at us and said we would not sleep at all if we watched the spooky TV show if we were already that scared. As I rolled out our sleeping bags by the fireplace, Stacey asked my parents if there were any haunted locations near our home and then threw a pillow at my head. Stacey and I were in Wilderness Survivors together where we sold cookies, slept under the night stars, and we often told spooky stories around the campfire. Stacey was as thrilled as I was to hear my parent's stories as they were often true or dealing with local legends. They were great at painting a picture of haunted places they heard about or visited. My mom told my dad to tell us about the haunted mill village cemetery in our neighborhood. My mom, Stacey, and I nestled down in the sleeping bags while my dad sat on the black and red bean bag chair. We heard the coal fireplace crackle and pop and saw the fire flicker on my dad's tanned skin while his blue eyes danced. He began to tell us his and his brother's experiences with the lady in white.

Dad's father died when dad was very young. Consequently, Dad attended several different mill village elementary schools as his mom struggled to secure a mill home for them. Finally, after his mother became a supervisor in the local mill, the two of them moved into their own mill village home that was a newly built home. He often reminisced about walking into the home for the first time, smelling new paint. I remembered seeing him smile as he recalled fondly when he stepped into the mill home, as a young boy, and looked up when sawdust blew in his eye. Dad's favorite mill village elementary school was Grenola Elementary in the original site which is now torn down. While attending Grenola, he heard and old story about a murdered schoolteacher that died during World War II.

Grenola School, circa 1913

I do not recall if the teacher actually taught my father as he spoke of her so fondly that it appeared, he knew her. Since Dad was born near the beginning of World War II, it is possible that she did teach my father, but he did not indicate that to be a fact. He described the lady as an attractive schoolteacher, a newlywed, with a kind smile and heartwarming demeanor. She moved into the mill village with her husband, and they started trying to have a baby right away. To everyone's excitement, the lovely and kind schoolteacher told the students that she was indeed with child! But the excitement did not linger as soon afterwards her husband was called to go to war. She was pregnant and home alone so all the neighbors agreed that she would be watched after by the neighborhood. Because of the mill's ongoing support of military troops, as the mill made most of the uniforms for the military during the war, the schoolteacher could continue living in the mill home and using the grocery store credit line. During a particularly dark winter night, a drifting burglar came into her home and robbed her. During the fight, her pregnant belly was injured, and she fell hitting her head. The neighbors heard screaming and ran to the home to find her in a pool of blood as she fell, and she suffered a severe head wound. The hospital doctors did all they could, but she lost the baby and then shortly afterwards, she died from complications of her injuries and blood loss. The people of the community called the Red Cross who contacted the military to notify her husband only to find out that he was a combat casualty of war the same day as her and the baby's death. Their deaths were in synchronicity. The community decided to bury her with her infant in her arms in the local cemetery.

Three days later, several neighbors reported seeing her just after dinner time before the sun went down, at the mill village grocery store. She was seen wearing the white gown she was buried in while standing in the checkout line to buy milk. When she went to the register to put the milk on her credit line for her baby The people that lived near the cemetery also told the police that they heard a baby crying and a saw a woman walking – more like floating – in the graveyard. When the police arrived at cemetery to investigate, they found bottles of milk on the cemetery plot where the schoolteacher and her baby were buried. The bottles of milk were full of milk where she felt she needed to feed her baby. Did she know that they both were dead? I have always felt that she could not bear to think that her baby died when she wanted to nurture it so badly.

Stacey and I were emotionally moved to tears, angered at the burglar for hurting the schoolteacher and baby, but we were hungry for more of the tale. My dad said that he felt the spooky story was to, "keep the kids out of the cemetery because teens often went into the graveyard to smoke cigarettes and even take a swig of alcohol or two."

Photography by
Leitreanna Brown

However, dad did say that his brother, who was a smoker and a drinker in his younger day, witnessed the lady in white. Josh claimed to feel like he was being watched every time he went to the cemetery to hide from his stepmom. He did not like being in the cemetery after dark but dared not show it to his friends as they would make fun of him. One night he was in the cemetery near the schoolteacher's graveside leaning against a tombstone while hanging out with friends. My dad often described his older stepbrother Josh to me. He loved his brother but described a young, stubborn teenager that often-learned lessons the hard way. My uncle at that time wore dark jeans that were rolled up at the ankle, wore high top tennis shoes, a white t-shirt where he kept a pack of cigarettes rolled into his short-sleeved shirt, and often threw his black leather jacket over his shoulder.

While the local teens were hanging out in the graveyard, one of the older guys had a pint of whiskey and offered to share with them. I often wondered if my uncle, the rebel that he was, took that pint to the cemetery, but my uncle never admitted to it. Dad said that, just as the sun was going down, my Uncle Josh took a swallow of the whiskey and then looked over his friend's shoulder and saw a woman floating near them while a faint cry of a baby slowly started to pierce their ears. No sound came out of their mouths even though they felt like they were screaming.

The boys, being terrified, picked up rocks and started throwing the rocks at the ghostly figure but since the sun was going down, they could not see the spirit well or see if their rocks made contact so they ran as quickly as they could all the way home. My dad told me that the next day, the boys and my uncle met after school in the cemetery and the rocks they threw were stacked on the schoolteacher's tombstone. Uncle Josh refused to go into the cemetery again even risking being caught with cigarettes as my grandmother, Johnnie Cogburn (my paternal grandmother) made him eat them if she caught him.

Just as mom and dad predicted, Stacey and I stayed up all night talking about the lady in white. Even though we had fun, played board games, and watched TV, we had a hard time falling asleep because our minds were captivated with the murdered schoolteacher's story and we both jumped every time the wind blew. Could she float into our sleep over? The neighborhood cemetery is at end of the street, it was possible! With every passing car's headlights, we were sure that the shadows they cast was the lady in white coming in the house to scare us and we did not have any rocks to throw. Stacey's mom came to pick her up shortly after we finally fell asleep. We were exhausted. After Stacey went home, I talked to my mom about the lady in white. My mind wandered back to the schoolteacher's ghostly story.

Mom told me that Mama Jenny and Gigi went to the cemetery to investigate the story as they often did with ghostly reports. Mom said that Mama Jenny and Gigi would never be afraid of a lady with a broken heart but rather would like to help her in some way which conditioned me to understand more about their mindset when they investigate. I felt very calm and curious after I discussed the lady in white case with my family. How different were Gigi and Mama Jenny since they were on their own during wartime and they could have easily had a similar fate? Determined to help the ghostly lady, the mother and daughter team investigated the cemetery to contact the lady in white. The reputedly beautiful apparition did not make an appearance for them and could not be heard. Sometimes some spirits can be seen by some people and not by others. Sometimes, the ghostly spirit is triggered by a significant time in their lives which causes them to haunt the locations of their earthly domain. During Gigi and Mama Jenny's investigation, the timing was not right, or it simply was not meant for them to see the specter.

My grandmother used a compass as an investigative tool where she would ask the ghostly figure to make the compass needle move. She did have needle movement but was not so sure if the spirit wanted to communicate. In addition, when they returned for another investigation, they brought candles with them when it was not windy outside and at the ladies' request, the candles were blown out. Gigi and Mama Jenny hoped for more obvious spiritual activity as with the mild reactions, it is possible that coincidence caused the responses and not actual spectral manipulation. The ladies agreed that the schoolteacher's spirit was near them in the cemetery as they felt her presence and her grief but overall, the case was benign and did not require intervention. Gigi and Mama Jenny was not in the investigation for the thrill of the hunt but rather their genuine interested in helping the mother and the baby. Mama Jenny and Gigi never discovered what happened to the lady in white's husband.

Where he was buried, where he was killed, or if he was every brought home to American soil is never known. This part of the story remains a mystery.

Years later, Mama Jenny was pleasantly surprised to learn I was interested in the lady in white story. Although my father and his mother found my interest disconcerting, Mama Jenny entertained my questions and curiosity. Mom told Mama Jenny that I was interested in the lady in white because it was heart breaking and I wanted to help her in some way which reminded her of her own interest in the case. My heart ached for the lady in white as she had such a lost love and it doomed her to wander. Mom knew that I would not stop until I had more information and I showed that I was not fearful of the ghosts as that was behind me. Remembering the details of the case with Gigi years prior, Mama Jenny felt that the schoolteacher's case was a good one for me to investigate since the exploration was mild in response. So, the two of them took me to the mill village grocery store where the ghostly schoolteacher was reported being seen on multiple occasions several years after her death as her spectral visitations continued from several days after her death until recently. Surely the schoolteacher was not still making her ghostly walk to care for her dead infant.

I wanted to ride my pink bicycle with a banana seat and spoke beads that clickety clacked when I pedaled my bike as I loved going to the store, but Mama Jenny insisted that I ride with her in her Pacer. We arrived at the Mill Village Grocery store, parked in the parking along the street in front the building and walked over past the beauty parlor. I could smell shampoo and all sorts of hair products swirling in the air. The beauty parlor a place I wanted to see and it was in the basement of the building. I wanted to go upstairs to the clothing store because they got a new shipment of bell bottom jeans, but our mission was to talk to Mr. Herbert and I fell behind Mama Jenny as she went into the store straight to the butcher shop where Mr. Herbert worked most often.

Mama Jenny asked Mr. Herbert, the grocery store owner, to tell me about his experience about the mill village cemetery with the lady in white's grave and milk bottles. Mr. Herbert smiled and greeted every customer, wore a white collared shirt, wore a white butcher's apron, kept a black grease pencil in his shirt pocket for writing on butcher paper, wore black slacks, and butcher's hat every day. He spoke to every person that came into the store and gave them a big pat on the back. He gave free $.01 bubble gum to each child that came through the door on Saturday mornings. The grocery store kept penny candy in an old butcher case and we often got small brown bags of candy if we helped our parents with their groceries. Although Mr. Herbert showed great hesitation, he continued with his personal account of the ghostly specter as he knew Mama Jenny and what she does so he knew there would be no doubting his word. Mr. Herbert said he was not the cash register clerk during the specter's sighting but was able to clearly see her from the butcher's area. One of the high schoolers was on the register. The ghostly woman had a stoic face, very pale skin, and was wearing a gown identical to the legend's description of her burial gown. As she approached the counter holding the milk, the only words she spoke were the credit line number for her family. Then she headed for the door. The cashier tried to stop her as Mr. Herbert ran towards the door because he felt like she was the beautiful schoolteacher, but she had vanished after going out the door. One of the cemetery grounds keepers found the milk on the schoolteacher's grave plot and returned it Mr. Herbert. Mr. Herbert's face showed fear, even when remembering the ghostly figure from many years ago, and he proceeded to cut the sharp cheddar cheese my grandmother ordered, wrapping it in butcher paper, and precisely tying the twine string without breaking eye contact with us and I knew every word he told us was the truth.

Over two decades later, after I married and moved to another home, I told my husband about the ghostly schoolteacher and her crying baby as my heavy heart still clung to one of the greatest love stories never told. Since I met the love of my life and he was a soldier, I clearly understood her heartache. Our love stories certainly ran parallel until hers came to a sudden tragic end. We drove out to my old family home to see the infamous cemetery so that we could scour the many tombstones to try and narrow down which one may be the final resting place for the lady in white, hoping we could have a personal experience or collect some evidence. If we were successful in making contact in any way, we knew Mama Jenny and my mom would be thrilled to see what we captured. We opened our equipment boxes and took out all our hand-held ghost hunting instruments deciding how we would move forward with our probe. We established a base line reading of the environment noting the temperature, the electronic fields, the weather, the time we started the investigating, and documenting any possible items that could contaminate our evidence when we review. Suddenly, after starting our electronic voice recording and asking for anyone in the cemetery to contact us, we heard a faint noise. We heard something pulsing. Even though there were textile facilities nearby, they had been shut down many years prior. We could not explain the heartbeat type sound.

It was a hot summer night with very little wind, and we experienced cold spots with temperatures varying up to seven degrees from one second to the next. The temperatures dropped every time we asked entities buried near our location to make contact and the temperature would always return to our base line temperature shortly afterwards. We felt as though we were being watched and followed as we walked through the graveyard continuously hearing that forever beating sound that engulfed us. People that live near the cemetery came to us and asked if we were there to pay respects to the lady in white. They claimed to have seen the her on many occasions, but they were certain and abruptly stated, that they did not hear a baby cry. The neighbors were very concerned that we would disrespect her in some way as they had developed an affection for her. We assured them that we were merely curious, and we would be sure to pick little flowers out of the clover and leave them on her grave like the local children have through the years. The schoolteacher who influenced so many students, looked forward to being a mother of her own child, and carried that desire from her life into infinity. Hopefully, the lady, her husband, and the baby were able to reunite. The murdered schoolteacher aka Lady in White remains a mystery.

Chapter 7

The Children's Home See-Saw

After dinner one night, our phone rang and my father was in his office pacing, talking to someone. After a while, my dad was put on hold, so my dad whispered to my mom something about a Children's Home needing our help. The Director, called and asked for assistance. I had several friends from school that lived in a children's home and were as close as brothers and sisters. I loved playing with them because they always shared their toys, enjoyed playing with everyone, and was good in school. I hoped to see some of my friends at the children's home, so I listened carefully. Dad told mom that the children's home was over hour away so I knew I would not see my friends, but I was interested in what was happening and why he needed to go. My dad lectured in schools and my mom often helped him. We had been to several dinners where mom and dad were recognized for helping schools, so I wondered if they were lecturing or if something else more serious was their purpose or mission.

Previously, Mom and Dad brought home some exciting playground equipment for one of my birthdays. I had a see-saw, swing set, and a whirl. The colorful swing had a metal slide, two plastic seats for swings, and a cart on the swing where you could sit on a bench and swing. I loved my swing set because it was safe, all my friends could play on it, and it gave me butterflies in my stomach when I swung high. The teeter totter was a long wooden plank attached to a bar and someone sat on each end. The kids bounced up and down on each end. The problem with see-saws is the danger. The older see-saws were wooden planks mounted on top of a concrete base. Kids occasionally banged their tailbone and experienced spinal injuries. If someone jumped off the one end, the other person on the other end fell. Kids pinched fingers and got splinters on see-saws, so we rarely used my see-saw. The whirl was more fun because four kids could sit on the seats arranged in an X formation and we had handles where we pushed and pulled to turn the whirl around. If we went too fast, someone could fall off, so we only used that equipment with supervision. I thought about my play equipment as I heard my dad tell my mom that a kid fell off the see-saw at the children's home. I saw mom's face and she looked like she was going to cry. She hid her face from me, and I realized that dad was whispering again on the phone with his contact. I wanted to know what was going on and who got hurt.

Finally, my dad got off the phone, so mom and I needed information about the call as our senses were on high alert. Mom and dad sent me to my room to talk so I reluctantly went into my room and waited until I could not bear to be left out of the situation, so I went back to dad's office. After I begged and pleaded for what seemed like ages, mom told me that someone jumped off a tall see-saw and allowed the other person on the other end to fall hard. It was a little girl; she fell so hard from the see-saw she broke her neck. I was ready to find whoever hurt that girl and get some playground justice but then it dawned on me that our mission was a paranormal investigation and the little girl was our objective. There were reports from people around the playground that they heard a see-saw squeaking like it was being played on, but nobody was there. Sounds coming from the playground started shortly after the little girl's death, so mom and dad were called to help. The fried chicken that I ate for supper flipped over in my stomach as my heart ached for the girl that may be spiritually still playing on that see-saw - forever falling. Dad was already in action mode, asking if I had gotten my homework, and luckily it was Friday night and I had done my homework for the weekend and he grabbed his professional cameras, lenses, and recording equipment. Mom got a thermos of hot chocolate and her bag of equipment, plus she got rain jackets since it was an uncommonly warm that evening for fall, so a shower was likely on the way. We were off to meet the Director of the Children's Home to figure out what was happening on that playground. I felt like I was able to help that kid since I was a kid and often played on playgrounds and I was trying to formulate questions for the spirits. Just as I decided on three questions for the investigation, my parents dropped a bomb on me. Dad looked in the rearview mirror to the back seat where I was, raised his strong, thick eyebrows and said that he did not want me getting out of the car. Mom, after putting on her red lipstick and fastening her long flowing black hair into a barrette, turned around to stop me from talking back to my father. She said that they felt like I needed to stay in the car while they talked and looked around.

I was livid that they would not trust me enough to help. Mom said that it was not a matter of not trusting me, it was a matter of not trusting the spirit as they did not know what they were dealing with yet. I said, "A kid will feel more comfortable talking to another kid especially if someone their age hurt them, and they want to make friends. It is hard to trust people when you have been hurt." My parents were not having it and I was to stay in the car without any arguments. I was so angry I decided to tune out my parent's conversation and I fell asleep in the back seat. What was the point of listening? Why didn't they leave me at home? I knew right away I was fooling myself. I did not want to be left at home because then I would not know anything about what happened to the girl on the playground. I laid down on the backseat and listened to the tires humming on the road. Mom and dad turned up the radio as they often did when they wanted to talk without my hearing their conversations in the front of the car. I fell asleep and dreamt of a playground with kids playing and I then watched a see-saw seat pop up abruptly, then heard screams ricochet throughout the playground. When the adults came running to the see who fell off the see-saw, I woke up suddenly.

The wheels of the car came to a stop and it woke me up because all I could hear was the radio playing. Since mom put a blanket over me when I fell asleep, I pulled the blanket over my head so they would leave me alone because I was really upset for being left out. As my dad got out of the car, I peeked through the blanket out the car window and I could see his dingo boots and the legs of blue jeans pacing outside. Finally, I saw another set of men's feet and I knew the person dad came to meet was there. Mom turned to me and told me she knew I was not asleep under the blanket and she reminded me I was to stay in the car and look after the vehicle. She knew I loved our car, the style, the smell, and the music, specifically the stereo sound. It was a black Thunderbird with suicide doors, leather seats that dad kept shiny and clean. The car radio sounded great in the back seat as the bass was deep and I could feel the seats reverberate the sound. I asked mom to keep the radio on and I would go back to sleep. She agreed and then kissed my forehead and got out of the car to meet up with my dad and the Director. I fell back asleep in the backseat of the car but woke up to a bright flash of light.

A storm was coming in and lightening was in a distance but still lighting up the entire night sky. Flashes of lightening became more frequent and I knew that we would be leaving soon. Who would want to walk around at night in the rain? I realized that I started feeling cold and I drew the crochet blanket closer around me so the cold rain coming down was cooling off the night air quickly. I felt my stomach flip again and I realized I was not upset like I felt I was earlier, but something was wrong with my abdomen. The nausea started getting worse and the storm's lightning and thunder intensified. Hot and cold chills started down my arms and legs so I knew I needed to go to the bathroom as I might be getting sick.

The clouds opened to a down pour. As I sat up, I saw legs and feet running in the rain as I knew mom, dad and the Director would be running to get out the rain. I was concerned with mom and dad did not come back to the car right away, I waited and did not see anyone. I finally decided to get out of the car. Suicide doors on the car opened the opposite direction than other car doors so I did not see the car coming. I looked up and I saw a girl a little older than me, with a panicked look on her face, looking back at me. She lambasted forward towards me and screamed, "NO, DO NOT GET OUT!"

Suddenly a car, speeding in the night rain, sped around our car as I was opening the door. They drove right through the ghostly image of the girl. I was opening the door out towards the street instead of sliding over and getting out on the sidewalk so I would have been hit by the speeding car if the spirit of the girl had not saved me. The ghostly girl had on an orange, plaid pantsuit with brown boots, but her hair was swirling around in brown locks like she was under water, so I knew she was a spirit.

Mom started screaming and ran toward the car with dad not far behind her. Swooping in to save me, mom and dad quickly got me, mom took me to the bathroom where I did, indeed, get sick. When I came out, dad dried me off from the rain in one of the rooms in the maintenance building of the orphanage, and we sat still while all three of us looked in shock of what transpired before our eyes. The Director came in, bid us a goodbye, and said he was headed back to his home on the other side of the orphanage. He thanked us for coming and said that he would talk to dad later. After the Director left, I asked if they saw the ghostly girl on the playground or if they heard the squeaking see-saw. Dad said that he found some type of pump on the ground that pumped rain out of the playground and he believed that was the source of the noise, however mom was not so quick to explain the whining noise of the pump as she heard it clearly before it started raining so there was no need for the pump to function. I knew my ghostly friend was at the playground because she saved me. She was lovely and she had determined my fate instantaneously becoming my eternal friend.

Decades later, my husband, children and I went back to the old playground site as I still had questions about the playground even though we were never called back to the Children's Home again as everyone was satisfied the pump made the noises heard around the playground. Now, the playground is simply a field by the road, that nobody uses. Some flowers have been planted and the grass is a deep shade of green showing that little shoes no longer trampled their footprints on the ground as they played. The playground is nothing but a memory. I heard the squeaking but did not see a pump as my dad told me about as a child. I did not see my ghostly friend either.

Before we made the trip to the playground, we checked the weather to make sure that no storms were coming so we did not have thundershowers on our trip. The field had flower gardens so the space for investigating was much smaller. Maybe the ghostly little girl was worried my middle school aged children would be frightened by her. If she knew that my children could see spirits, she would not have been concerned. Maybe she did not recognize me, so she did not make herself known. Maybe the specter had moved on. Who knows for sure? Maybe the only purpose that night was to save me from the same fate she had which was to lose her life on that playground. When I went there as a child, I wanted to make friends that night and indeed I had made friends with a ghostly little girl that knew how to take care of her friends. Maybe the spirit of the girl knew that her playmate on that fateful day did not mean to hurt her when he jumped off the see-saw, and she forgave him leaving no unfinished business in her soul. She seemed friendly and positive since she helped me when I needed help. I knew the truth about the playground, and I will never forget the see-saw girl who saved me. There are many times as we walk through this life that we have spirits, ancestors, and familiars where they protect you from an unknown danger. If you have an encounter like this, honor it for the good intentions that originated their actions.

Chapter 8

The Hat Man

Around 1931, my great grandmother, Guynell, was a young, single mother as her husband became ill and was in hospitals most of his life. She moved onto the Mill Village after acquiring a job in one of the first textile mills in her town. She was thrilled to have gotten a home for her and her young daughter, Virginia (my grandma). Guynell had polio as a child and was considered crippled by many doctors. She was told she would never have children and lost several sons with a doctor trying to help deliver them, until she finally found a midwife that could help her deliver her only surviving child, Virginia. The pride she felt getting the textile job that ultimately gave her and her daughter a home, helped heal her broken heart.

Guynell had fallen in love with a musician that loved women even more than music, so her marriage did not give her or her daughter any stability or love. Guynell desperately needed her job in the mill needed since she resulted to enrolling Virginia in a children's home for a while until she could do better for her daughter.

The mother and daughter were celebrating moving into their home, so they decided to take a walk and take in the sights. They met their neighbors and enjoyed their friendly neighbors' greetings. They saw their neighbors taking their laundry to the laundry truck and get ice from the ice box truck which was exciting since moving into the mill village offered the two of them many luxuries that they had not had much of before. Guynell walked, and Virginia rode on her small bicycle as they saw many neighbors in the area. Before leaving home, Virginia attached cards in the wheel spokes and the bike rattled as she pedaled. They rounded the corner of their street, Pine Street, as the streetlights starting to come on. Virginia's bicycle twinkled as she pedaled through the streetlights.

Neither Guynell nor Virginia saw the man approaching them. Previously, he was not there but now he appeared in front of them as large as life. He had piercing eyes, a hardened shadowed, wrinkled face, wore a long, dark coat which was too hot for the time of the year, and he wore a large, wide brimmed black hat. They saw the male entity lock his eyes on them, so Guynell instructed Virginia to go around to avoid him. They tried to go around him and no matter how much they moved to go around, the figure came straight like he just came out of the darkness and was on a specific mission. Even though Guynell told Virginia to go around him, the two still looked up and he was standing there but this time he spoke. He told them, "Somebody is going to die tonight."

The tall dark figure reached out and touched Guynell with his spindly, boney hand, and a chill ran down her arm to her small, weak legs. They walked past him in extreme alarm, so scared because Guynell could not imagine why in the world would he tell her someone is going to die that night plus he said the statement in front of her young daughter. She jerked her arm away, turned suddenly and got away from him. Guynell's legs continued to tingle as she topped the hill toward their home, but she could not be distracted by tingling legs right now as she was frightened to the bone. When they both passed another home, they came to a large azalea bush where they felt they had some hidden coverage, so they turned around and the hat man was gone. When they look back, the man should have been in another streetlight that they had passed before. They never saw him go under the streetlight and just as quickly as he appeared, he disappeared without a trace.

The next day, Guynell and Virginia were outside sweeping the walkway looking around to see if they saw any signs of the hat man. As Guynell swept the sidewalk, she noticed that she did not feel the morning aches and pains in her legs. Her mind never stopped thinking about that man with the hat. She wondered why he said someone was going to die last night. They saw several of their neighbors going about their day. Mrs. Jones, who baked and sold cakes, soups, stews, and lunch box meals for workers in the mill, lived on the left side of their home. They asked Mrs. Jones if she saw a tall man wearing a long dark coat and dark hat walking the street last night and she said she indeed see the man. Other neighbors also confirmed witnessing the unknown man. Finally, the Sunday school teacher came up the street with a horribly grim look on her face. She gave the information that someone in the neighborhood died during the night. Mrs. Smith, who lived 3 houses past Mrs. Jones, had been sick for several months. She got up during the night and died in her hallway as if she were walking toward the door.

Just thinking back, Virginia wondered if the hat man had disappeared off Pine Street then went to Mrs. Smith to take her soul away as a grim reaper. She thought again about her legs and wondered if a grim reaper had the ability to heal her. What an interesting and terrifying thought. Truly, Guynell had mysterious questions that remained unanswered. A week later, another person saw the hat man, and again the same night, there was a death in the neighborhood. Eventually, the news got back to Guynell and she was determined to get to the bottom of the mystery as if it were one to solve as to who or what she experienced on Pine Street.

Virginia, on the other hand, also felt that when that he came face to face with her mother, he healed her, and she was grateful. Guynell worked with renewed strength and Virginia was thrilled to have been able to spend more quality time with her mom and it was an answer to her prayers. Mama Jenny said she always wondered who that hat man was, and if he a death Angel, if there is such a thing. Why he told them why he was there, remains a mystery. Mama Jenny told me that she saw the man with the hat she called him the hat man, several times, and they started researching trying to identify the mysterious dark messenger. Through the years, Mama Jenny said, they never figured it out. Each time the hat man was seen, someone died the next day. Mama Jenny and mom took up the hunt after Gigi died but, the mystery was never solved. Eventually, the hat man sightings were few and the fear subsided. The memories of the hat man on the mill village remain with Mama Jenny and my mother. Many people over the years have reported sightings of the hat man, followed by horrible accidents, injuries, and illnesses afterwards. My family experienced the hat man and lived to tell their experiences.

My husband and I went to Pine Street, to see if we could figure out what happened in 1931 when my Mama Jenny, and Gigi, started their journey researching the hat man. The street name was changed but we were able to locate, not only the home that Mama Jenny lived in, but the home of Mrs. Smith. We found the home but did not get any paranormal readings in the road or sidewalk. Since the home is occupied, we did not disturb the current owners as we felt that they would be alarmed about their wellbeing if we knocked on the door and asked them if they saw a Hat Man that is also a grim reaper. We continued researching the family members of Mrs. Smith in hopes that we could get an interview with one of them. All of Mrs. Smith's family members were deceased except her daughter in law who retired from the tax collector's office many years prior. We were not able to find her daughter in law as she moved when she retired. Even if we did, we were pretty sure that she would not be aware of the details her mother in law's death. Through mill records, we discovered that Mrs. Smith's young sons took an employment contract with the mill when their father died so, since her sons worked in the mill, she was able to stay in the home and her son's checks were docked for rent. Her youngest son did not marry until after his mother died therefore the daughter in law would not know any details of Mrs. Smith's death.

Since it had been too long since the hat man appeared in 1931, we decided to ask the local spirits of the area if they had any knowledge. Spirits would not be bound by flesh and blood limitations. We were able to speak with several spirits that were in the area by paranormal equipment and through mediumship tactics. These nearby spirits had not seen the hat man, or they did not admit they had. Interestingly, spiritual activity around Pine Street was rampant. In fact, one of the most severe hauntings we ever experienced was only one block away from Pine Street. We wonder if the hat man was drawn to the area due to spiritual activity. Another way of looking at it, maybe the spiritual activity was caused by a possible grim reaper being present for so long during the 1930s? Again, the mystery remains within the spirit realm.

LEITREANNA BROWN

Chapter 9

Ghostly First Kiss

While my husband and I were working on our website for our paranormal investigative teams, we received a message from Gary, someone interested in learning how to do paranormal investigation and felt he was ready to join a team. When we met with the young man, we were enchanted with his eagerness to learn, his curiosity for the unknown, and his readiness to contribute to the team. Gary met our Family Spirit paranormal team and also Paranormal PROS where family members investigate with other members selected to participate. Gary completed official training for paranormal investigations and organized his equipment. Our team met several times to do training so that everyone would have known what to do, how to do it, and who would be their investigation buddy as we never investigate alone.

During Gary's last training session, he offered a very interesting location for our team to investigate. The site was a family member's home, which previously had been a Director's house on the mill village in a small town a few hundred miles from our training headquarters. We accepted the offer to investigate and we scheduled the date.

When we arrived, we discovered to our amazement that the home was bigger than we expected due to several renovations. The home was originally the home of the director of the local textile mill so we knew it would be large. After the mill started to struggle financially, the home had been renovated and converted into a children's home for youngsters with mental or physical challenges and the children's home housed, educated, and trained the kids. Unfortunately, it was not well funded. When the community fell on hard times, it was difficult for the caregivers of the home to provide good care. Many of the children were abandoned, therefore, the caregivers had an even more difficult task. Where would they go?

After the children's home closed it sat vacant for a long period of time, until Gary's family purchased it. As they had been in the antique business, they kept all their favorite pieces. All the extra space of this new home was ideal for all the cherished antiques they collected. We were thrilled to investigate the historic home, spread out into various teams, use every piece of our equipment, and research the home's history further.

We arrived at the home around 3:00 pm on a hot summer's day. When we drove through the circled driveway, we got out of our truck and stared at the old southern home realizing it was a perfect portrait of Americana. The large white pillars on the front porch dwarfed the small, black front door. Roses and green border grass lined the circular driveway until the driveway reached the home. The circular drive ended at the brick sidewalk. The garden followed the house on both sides of the brick sidewalk and was full of large, green hostas that ended at the steps to the porch. We wanted to see more of the yard, so we walked all the way around the house taking in the beauty of the historic home. The outdoor kitchen in the back yard was remarkable with a bricked walkway and patio and huge brick stove that formed into a chimenea.

The hot sun was still blazing down on us, so we decided to move all the gear inside then venture back out later in the afternoon. Sometimes, we cannot make plans about what we will do at locations because the investigation will set our night in action and take over our thoughts, actions, and reactions. But we hoped to see more of the beautiful gardens. Avoiding the scorching sunlight, we hurried our pace to get all the equipment in the home. Matthew took charge immediately showing each paranormal team member where he wanted the cameras, wiring, and other equipment. Working in teams, we set up all our tripods, ran all our cords for the night vision cameras and monitor, set all of our audio recorders in their locations, set up our command center, tested all equipment, then took a break to see if anyone had questions. As Matthew performed a walkthrough of the home to check all equipment and make sure all safety precautions were taken, he taped down any cords, marked all investigation locations, and passed out replacement batteries for equipment.

I spoke to the homeowners. Gary and his family did not report any paranormal claims at the home. Our presence there was solely an opportunity to investigate in a large space for our team's experience and training purposes. Everyone was excited and ready to see what the home would show us. We hypothesized that the granite and rock under the home, the stream (body of water) in the backyard, the antiques in the home were three ways that spiritual activity could be present. We completed our preliminary walk through and went down to the basement to look at the huge rock. The rock required investigators to climb about six feet to sit on the ridge which gave whomever sitting on the stone, an opportunistic view of the entire basement. The stone was about ten-foot high and covered in dried, red mud. The entire flooring of the basement was dried red mud also. I was tremendously intrigued to see if we would find any supernatural activity in the basement. The Stone Tape Theory is one where residential spiritual energy can be present if stone, granite, or limestone is present to capture the energy. We found granite and limestone on the property in the basement and around in the yard. Another theory is that a body of water can create energy as the water flows, which can give enough power for a paranormal entity to manifest. Paranormal attachment to a possession is a very old but accurate theory that spirits can attach themselves to their former material possessions. Many psychiatrists, psychologists, scientists have researched the theory of the eternal soul and if it can bond to its familiar environment. With all the antiques in the home, we acknowledge that antique stores often get stock for their stores by attending estate sales and liquidation auctions which is a perfect opportunity for a spiritual attachment to bond with a material possession that is then sold to an unsuspecting customer. Would these antiques, rocks or bodies of water give us supernatural activity? We hoped so.

The foyer had immaculate hardwood floors with a beautiful clear coated finish. The oak circular table in the center of the foyer was home to a tall, thin, oriental vase that displayed silk, orchid flowers the same type and shade as the flowers painted on the vase. Every room of the home had ornate lighting. The parlor had exquisite crystal chandlers; the foyer was lit by wall sconces with special electric light bulbs that flickered like candles. The kitchen had a woven wicker ceiling fan with every sort of cast iron cooking pan hanging from the ceiling by a mounted, cast iron, pot rack over the sink.

Every bedroom of the home had heavy four poster beds of different styles. Looking around each bedroom, I noticed pieces of wooden furniture of various colors of oak, pine, and maple. The variety each room displayed was exciting. One room theme was pale pink where the curtains were pale pink chiffon, the comforter and pillows were various shades of pink and the antique mirror was adorned with a pale pink ribbon. The bedroom across the hall was vibrant and vastly different than the other as the entire room was animal print. The curtains were leopard print with satin finish. The comforter was zebra print and the walls displayed hand carved African masks.

After we finished our water break, our hypothesizing about what we may discover with the investigation, and had our organization meeting where we set up the timeframes and locations that each pair of investigators would follow, we started the investigation to dig in and see what this historical, stunning home may have in store for our team. As we walked through the home back to the command center, I caught myself being mesmerized wondering about the history and mystery of the home, furniture, and décor.

We officially started the investigation at 7:00 pm. We saw that the heavy curtains, when closed, prevented any reflections for the outdoor sun to come into the home. We did not want sun flares, flashes of light and glares on our photographs and footage. Luckily, we were able to get an early start before it got dark. At first, all the investigators were focusing on their investigative style and techniques as we had a new investigator, Gary, on board and everyone was a bit self-conscious. We did not see, feel, or hear much paranormal activity in the first two hours. My husband and I discussed at length the possibility of our ten-year-old son, Elijah, who had amazing psychic abilities, joining us for the team's investigation. Elijah has seen spirits since he was a toddler and we were teaching him how to deal with his mystic capabilities. Elijah was chomping at the bit to investigate the former children's home and maybe this case would be a good opportunity for him. We called Nina and asked if she would bring Elijah to the site.

When they arrived, Elijah produced a kit of paranormal equipment that he had made himself. He had a notebook ready, prepared for the night. Nina stayed with us to watch Elijah, and to see what this phenomenal home would show us spiritually. After we gave him a snack, some water, and a rundown of the investigation sites, we allowed him to test his techniques in the foyer of the home. The foyer opened to a parlor and large formal living room. The crystal chandeliers were impressive but problematic because if we accidently used a flash when he took photos, the glare could cause false images on the photos that could be misinterpreted. Elijah took note of all the technical points we gave him. By the look on his face, he seemed aggravated with all the "dos and don'ts" we were giving him, so we gave him some quiet time to think and progress. He took the electronic thermometer and took a base reading of the temperature in the room. He noted the temperature on the night vision camera footage and the audio recorders for our case records. He then held his hand out, and said, "Hey I know you are here and are scared to talk to us. I am a kid too so you can talk to me."

Suddenly I remembered my investigation on the playground at the Children's Home when I was a child about the same age. He was getting more of an opportunity than I had at the same age. I hoped I was not mistaken for giving him a chance but since he had ghostly experiences on his own, frequently, it was more important to show him how to handle these experiences. I was thinking about my experiences at his age, when suddenly, Elijah got a meek response with this thermometer where the temperature got colder at his request for response.

We turned off the air conditioning and asked Elijah to repeat his process. We didn't want to measure the temperature in a home where the AC system would come on and affect our evidence. He asked if the spirit was a child, and the temperature got colder then returned to the base temperature. He asked if the child died when he or she was very young, and the temperature got noticeably colder in the room then returned to normal. He asked if the spirit was a girl or boy and she indicated girl by making the room get colder. Gary was mesmerized as he watched a child, unafraid of the supernatural encounter, use all types of tools to communicate with the unseen spirit. We turned on a ghost box and the female spirit indicated that she died due to stepping on a nail then her jaws locked, and she could not open her mouth. We recognized the symptoms the female spirit described as tetanus which is also called lockjaw. Nina, Elijah, and I felt jaw pain followed by a headache, so the ghost box session validated our psychic sense of an illness dealing with the jaw and head. Tetanus is a serious infection caused by Clostridium tetani. Tetanus creates bacterium that produces a toxin that affects the brain and nervous system, leading to stiffness in the muscles. If Clostridium tetani spores are deposited in a wound, the neurotoxin interferes with nerves that control muscle movement. This child died a horrible death which nowadays can be easily treated. Gary, moving with a sense of urgency, ran to the family office to see if he could find any historic ledgers of the specter child we were speaking with. Elijah was emotionally moved by the child's details of her death, so we decided to interrupt the investigation to give him a break and go to another location within the home.

In the next location, the female spirit followed us and continued to talk very quickly and excitedly with Elijah as she was not finished talking to him. Elijah was happy to hear from her and seemed calmer and we realized we were being overprotective of his emotions as he was handling the entire process maturely. We again interrupted his investigation because we wanted to see if any other spirits were there and moved Elijah to a different investigation spot in the home. Again, the female spirit continued to talk to Elijah but changed the subject talking about how she liked his equipment, she complimented him on his shirt which was a superhero shirt, and again complimented Elijah saying she found him to be attractive. Gary came back to our investigation to report that he found information on several children at the home but could not verify the attendance of the child spirit we were speaking with. Gary was stunned to discover the child spirit, flirting with Elijah telling him he was a nice person, a very cute boy and she said she wanted to play with him. Gary found a ball and tried to roll it to an unseen entity giving her the opportunity to roll it back. Instead, since I was sitting near Elijah as I always did when he investigated, my K2 meter detected that a magnetic field was near Elijah's shoulder. It moved to his neck, then his cheek. Finally, he felt a small amount of pressure on his cheek and then his lips and he knew that the young ghostly girl had given him a kiss which, was Elijah's first kiss. The K2 meter was blinking as high as the lights registered and flashed like a disco light. When he focused his eyes after the spirit's kiss, he saw the ghostly girl, wearing a long burgundy dress with flowers, shoes that came to her ankles, and sported a ponytail. He said that her smile was heartwarming and wondered how long the child's spirit tried to speak to people coming in and out of the home without being seen. She left our location after she kissed Elijah and we wondered where she went. We continued to investigate other spots in the home realizing we had little over an hour before meeting back in the parlor with all the team members. We eased our way to the basement to investigate the rock.

After the ghostly child left our location, other investigators were approached by the talkative, excitable young female spirit. She went to the kitchen and moved the wooden spoons in the jar on the counter for two of our investigators. One encounter surprised Rosalyn, one of our seasoned investigators. Rosalyn decided to eat dinner with her family and brought a Styrofoam cup of sweet tea from dinner to the investigation. She had the cup with a lid and straw in her large tote bag with wide side pockets where she also kept her ghost investigation equipment. She noticed that the straw kept going up and down in the cup. Rosalyn called all members to her location, so all the investigators gathered around with recording devices as we watched the mischievous little ghost girl try to steal sweet tea. The spirit child was having loads of fun talking to everyone, and even tried to get herself a few swallows of sweet tea just like a typical child would do.

We all felt that the sweet tea moment would be one we would never forget, we did not get any evidence at the basement rock or anywhere else in the home, so we wrapped up all the equipment, boxed our belongings, and loaded it into our vehicles. Gary and our team spoke with the Gary's family and told them we would have footage to show them. I really feel indebted to that precious, young, ghostly girl who gave my sweet son a wonderful memory of leading a paranormal investigation and getting his first kiss. Elijah knew the spirit child was there in the room the entire time as he felt her presence but knew she was too young and nervous to speak up, and he gently persuaded her to communicate with us. I was proud of Elijah's ability to psychically feel the spirit in the room, become adaptive by using the thermometer for something a little different than what it was designed to do, and then phrase his words to her to keep a genuine connection. Nina, Matthew, and I were proud of Elijah and his initiative.

Elijah was chatty all the way home as he was exhilarated and interested to see what the evidence presented. The next day we scoured through all the evidence and found lots of spectacular footage, photos, and audios. When children deal with the paranormal, they are open minded and inventive. Some theories that warn against children being involved with the paranormal, assume kids just cannot distinguish between what is reality and what is fantasy. They keep an open mind and give children the creative license to continue their friendly ghost experiences. Elijah has seen and heard spirits since he was old enough to express himself to us as a toddler. If we did not listen and give validity to his experiences, he would not have had the ghostly child's encounter proving his abilities were authentic and genuine. As an investigating team, it was at this point that the members of the team themselves can advance and possibly hinder an investigation. It was at this time that for future investigations, we would have moments where we would break up to age and gender teams to allow spirits the comfort and freedom to speak to someone that they felt more comfortable with.

Chapter 10

Bloody Thursday

When I became a new mother, I purchased a small wooden home in Honea Path, South Carolina. The home was reasonably priced and within a thirty-minute to forty-minute drive of three larger cities where I could get a good job. I felt I was being a shrewd parent getting the best of both worlds for my family where we could live a small-town life, but I could take advantage of a career path that a larger city offers. I had no idea this small wooden home a little larger than 1200 square ft would give me memories that would change my view of life and death.

I selected the house by looking at the map choosing a small town halfway between my job and my parents' home. I drove around the town looking for "FOR SALE" signs in front of homes. After driving a while, I took a break and ate at the local diner that features a meat with three vegetables as their blue-plate special. I mentioned to the waitress about my mission of looking for a cheap house between work and my parents so that I would have help with my baby and also more job opportunities in case I had to make a sudden career change. When you are a single parent, you think about the unknown variables with money and stability even more than you would if you had a partner to help with the burden of being a parent. The waitress came back with information from the kitchen staff that there was a darling little wooden house on the mill village for sale by owner. I hurried my meal down, grabbed my sweet tea to go, scooped up my baby in her carrier. Our new home might be literally just around the corner.

When I drove up to the house, I saw the for sale by owner sign hammered into the lawn. The grass was nearly as tall as the sign. The porch had chipped blue paint on the cement. The white wooden rails were small and basic. The mill village I grew up on did not look as deficient as the one I was at now. I looked around the neighborhood and saw that just behind the house was a boarding house. On the other side of the boarding house was the Chiquola Textile Mill. It was still running although it looked like it needed to be condemned. A feeling of sorrow come over me which I had not experienced with other mills. Somehow it felt like once you start working there you could never really leave. I personally had never worked in a textile mill although several of my close family members had. I heard stories about how they never called out of work unless there were extreme circumstances. I grew up listening to how close friends worked in the mill and lived near each other and I wondered if the workers in the Chiquola Mill had similar fond memories of friendship. I called the number on the for-sale sign and the owners agreed to meet with me immediately. We decided to wait until the next day as it would be dark when we did the walk through of the house by the time they arrived.

To say the current owners of the home were motivated to sell is an understatement. When I met them the next day, they said I could move in right away and set an amazingly cheap rental price then waved the pet deposits. The option to rent to own was added to the rental contract and I was set to move in. While the homeowner was wrapping up her documents, I reminded her to add my two cocker spaniels to the contract, so she was making changes, initialing them, and creating me a copy with her carbon copy paper. Her husband took me aside and I finally heard him speak. He never opened his mouth the entire time I had talked with his wife, the realtor and rental manager. He told me that the home had been a nightmare for them. His exact words were that "anything and everything that could go wrong with the home happened". They had a water pipe burst in the basement efficiency apartment and it ran for days running up their water bill. They had a tree limb fall on the house damaging the roof, and the plumbing under the kitchen sink fell out. He mentioned that he never understood the basement – someone started renovating as an efficiency apartment years ago, but they suddenly stopped leaving lots of unfinished work. He listed several other unfortunate repairs that needed to be conducted but, in the end, he said, when he fixed the repair himself, he always got hurt in some unexpected way. He showed me gashes on his knuckles from paint cans, a broken toe from a ladder and was about to show me his other hand's injuries when he realized his statements to me and said, "That is what happened to us while we owned the home. I am sure that it will not be as hard on you."

His wife caught the last statement and glared at him to be quiet. Beggars cannot be choosers, plus I had already signed the rental contract and planned to rent to own so it was too late to back out now. If my math were right, and my budget accurate, I could afford to have satellite TV while living in this home! The baby and I were going to live the high life!

While I was moving in, I had several close friends and family helping me. Mama Jenny bought me a used refrigerator and a new sofa, and mom gave me linens for my bed. When we arrived at the house, we had been on the road a while so everyone had to use the bathroom. Some people used the bathroom upstairs and others used the one downstairs in the efficiency apartment. Even though the efficiency apartment was not complete, the bathroom shower and toilet were installed. Everyone seemed to flush the toilets around the same time, and it sounded like the toilet on an airplane where you felt it would be easy to be sucked down the drain. Everyone undergoing the ferocious commode flush gave a startled shout when they experienced the whoosh. Next, everyone wanted some water. One of my friends washed his hands in the kitchen sink and prepared a glass of water when the water stopped up. He got the plunger out of the bathroom and after the second plunge, the PVC pipe under the kitchen sink fell out spilling water all over the kitchen linoleum and all over our feet.

My seven-month-old baby, Mia, was asleep in the living room and missed the unfortunate series of events. Luckily, the hardware store sold whatever it was that was needed to fix the sink and my dad had it under control in about forty-five minutes. I was nursing Mia in the rocking chair in the living room looking around at the bare walls wondering what on earth I had done to myself by getting financially saddled with the home. I reminded myself that I had cheap rent and I could easily save up and make a housing change if needed but that contract may be harder to deal with. The homeowner and her sad, scared little husband gave me suspicious feelings that I needed to watch them closely. After we assembled my bed and got all my belongings, as few as there were, in the house, I said my goodbyes to everyone and decided to take a shower then head to bed. I knew I threw my back out during the move and the only solution that could help me now would be to lay down flat and relax completely. Mia and I ate a snack, took our baths, and headed for bed. I grabbed my baby, my two cocker spaniels and fell asleep quickly in a puppy pile in my bed as we had a busy day with the move. Abruptly, I woke up hearing footsteps in the efficiency apartment below. It was two in the morning and someone was downstairs. Desperately searching for a weapon, I dashed to the kitchen, grabbed the heaviest item I could find, my wok, and I readied myself to defend my family. I left my female cocker spaniel, Demi, with Mia, and headed downstairs with my wok and male cocker spaniel, Picasso, to defend my daughter and myself from whatever lurked in the dark. While going down the steps, I did not realize how dark the basement was. I turned around and opened the door to my bedroom so the light would show through the door. When I turned around, A small dark figure run by uncommonly fast, so I doubted my eyesight. I backed up the stairs and ran to Mia. She was still asleep. Picasso and Demi got on the foot of the bed, looking around the room, and I held my baby and my wok while sitting on my knees in the bed wondering what to do next. Then, I decided to make a move. I put on shorts under my night gown, put on flip flops, grabbed my baby and my dogs, and headed to my car. I locked all of us tightly in the car and started the engine. I drove around both sides of my house shining the lights on the windows to see if I saw someone. Demi and Picasso, the cocker spaniels, looked out the car windows trying to make sense of the darkness and whatever was banging around in my house. Finally, after waiting and watching, I saw that nobody came out of the home, no shadows or movement broke the light of the headlight beams, and I figured I was being paranoid. I unloaded my car, went back into the house, locked all the doors, and we went back to bed. I was never so glad to go back to sleep as that day was truly taxing. I doubted my senses after that night as I was sure that what my dogs and I heard and reacted to was real but what could I do? I did not have any answers. All I could do is wait to see what happened next.

My mom and Mama Jenny came by to see me a few days later, on their way to the shopping mall. They passed through Honea Path to go to the favorite shopping mall, so they stopped in. They brought me casserole dishes and pans that I needed for the kitchen. The wooden paneling in the kitchen made my skin crawl. I was going to take measures to make the kitchen look updated very soon. I made progress setting up the home and gladly showed them Mia's polished, dark, wooden crib, with a pink teddy bear comforter and bumper pads. The matching, dark, wooden rocking chair was positioned on the right side of her crib. The small wooden dresser, and chest of drawers was not a perfect match as they were lighter wood, but they completed the bedroom and I felt accomplished. Mia always comes first and with her room set up, my anxiety from the move diminished to some extent. The living room décor was thrift store rescues that gave the home an antiquated but unique flair. The living room, even though it was nothing special, gave me an escape as the large TV, satellite dish, and comfy sofa Mama Jenny gave me was my escape. My job as a creative arts teacher required me to deal with children, parents, and teachers all day. When I was home, I could rest in solitude once the baby was asleep. Alone time helped me choreograph dances, organize dance or theater performances, read books, or simply be a lazy person and not think of anything but what the TV was playing.

In time, the only actual happiness I experienced was watching Mia grow and develop. I looked at the home and felt like a failure. When I was at work, I was enthralled with the children's excitement for dance and theater, but my happiness was short lived as I faced personal challenges with the job that stole my joy along with a house that made me feel uneasy. The monotony of fighting traffic to get from school to school three times per day made me nervous. Teachers' roles changed, I had to adapt to the changes each new teacher wanted, and I faced the gut-wrenching dilemma of lack of job security. The state grant I was paid from was being threatened by new state legislators, so my job security was in jeopardy. If the grant money were eliminated, I would need to find another job.

I was two weeks into the new school year when I finalized the performances for the year. Based on cost alone, the school districts I worked with selected my submissions. I was approved to purchase puppets for the middle school classes. The elementary school and primary school would be able to see their performances. I waited more than three weeks for the approvals so finally I could rest my mind and focus on getting ready for the performances scheduled for the end of the year.

I got home just before the rain started. Mia and I were glad to be home as she was all smiles and I felt relief when I kicked my shoes off. I turned on some big band music, lit some jarred candles, put Mia in her play pen, and started making some stir fry vegetables. Since Mia was sitting up, talking, crawling, and eating food, I needed the play pen for her when I was cooking. Mia loved all the vegetables and I had a food processor to prepare her food. While I was cooking dinner, Mia was sitting in her playpen and I heard her trying to speak like she does when she speaks to mom and me. I took two steps backwards from the stove to look in the living room on Mia. My baby was holding her hands up toward the left of the playpen like she does when she wants to be picked up. She was looking at something I could not see and interacting with it! I stood in disbelief watching my child wanting to be picked up by an unseen entity and the closer I walked toward the playpen, my daughter turned her head away as if the entity was walking away from the playpen because I was coming towards it. I snatched my baby up out of the play pen, turned the stove off, grabbed my dogs, my purse, Mia's baby bag and headed to mom's house. I had to work the next day and it would mean over an hour commute one way for me in heavy traffic very early in the morning, but I needed help right away. My cell phone needed to be charged, Mia was screaming bloody murder as I am sure I startled her, the dogs were jumping from seat to seat in the car, and I was nearly out of gas. I pulled into Dill's gas station, got out to pump gas, and wondered how much money I had for gas. I burst into tears. Everything was spiraling out of control. Even though I had been exposed to ghosts throughout my life, now I had one in my house that I couldn't see but my baby could, and it freaked me out! Is this fiend in my house making all the bad things happen in the home? Is she or he trying to run us out like the landlord's husband explained? My mind went back to the moment the landlord's husband showed me the injuries on his hands, I wondered will that be next, and will they try to hurt Mia? What was I going to do? The only thing I can do is go to mom and Mama Jenny. I pumped the amount of gas I could afford as some of my classes had not started yet so I had an unexpected cut in pay, which was another source of pain and frustration in my life. I headed to my mom and Mama Jenny with a prayer in my heart begging God to protect my baby and show me what is going on in the new home that I now hated.

I arrived at mom and dads to discover mom was on the porch waiting for me. How she always knew I was upset I will never know but she was always on time with her support for me when I need it. She met me in the yard getting Mia out of the car seat. My ego suddenly kicked me in the back of the head because now it occurred to me that a spirit just ran me out of my own home. I had been involved in paranormal cases since childhood and now a spirit that interacted with my baby caused me to panic and drive all the way home to mom and dad. Was I so inept that I couldn't handle a haunting on my own? In my own defense, the spirit was interacting with my baby. I waited to tell mom and wondered if she would think I didn't learn anything from all the cases our family dealt with over the years. Dad went on extreme cases and worked with clergy to assist in exorcisms. I did not stand my ground at all!

After dinner, when the house quieted down, I told my mom what happened. She called Mama Jenny and the grandmas were overjoyed that Mia had spiritual gifts like the other ladies of our family. I was not at all thrilled. First, I was a single parent of a child not even old enough to speak that has psychic abilities. We lived in a haunted home with something that I had not seen yet. Why wasn't I able to see this spirit? Was there a reason? The only reason I could think of is was the spirit was deliberately not wanting me to know what or who it is. My imagination ran wild and I became more and more concerned for my baby at every moment.

Mama Jenny got on the phone with me and told me to sit down for a while and listen. Mom brought me a glass of sweet tea and I got my first lesson about being a mother to a psychic child. Mama Jenny said, "Darling, sometimes the spirit world shows us things about ourselves and the people around us. It is not by our choice or timing." I realized she was right and then Mama Jenny continued, "Now you understand how your mother and father felt when you saw the man in blue. You see why your dad wanted to protect you from anything paranormal because he felt helpless to protect you."

I knew my grandmother was wise, but I felt like I was talking to a sage. Mom said, "You stay the night with us, get some good rest, leave Mia here instead of taking her with you to work or to daycare, and we will meet you half way when you get off work. We will talk more then. Remember we are all in this together."

I felt like I temporarily had the weight of the world off my shoulders. I was getting my second wind and going back to that mill house in Honea Path tomorrow to figure out the paranormal puzzle that somehow was dumped in my lap by way of searching for cheap housing. In the past, I often saw nothing happens by coincidence and I looked forward to discovering the bigger picture of the house in Honea Path. In my heart, I felt that a very dark secret would be uncovered.

Mia, my sweet baby, was turning one soon. She was walking at eleven months and shortly afterward she was potty trained. I was so excited to be rid of diapers! She had the brightest smile with adorable dimples and was the light of my life. I grew accustomed to seeing her talk to an unseen entity and from the positioning of Mia's arms I could tell that the spirit was rather short. Mia loved watching princess movies over and over with her invisible friend. When I put Mia in her playpen, Mia's toys that she dropped or threw, often ended up within her arms reach so that she could recover them herself. At least there was a bright side. My poor dogs often growled at unseen specters and I assured them that we were watching the entities together. When the spirits in the home were particularly busy at night, we always had very weird events that followed. One night my brown sunhat was on the post of my dresser and I found it on top of the microwave. Later that night I found what looked like an infant kitten on the porch. It had the smallest face and very fine fur. Something inside me said for me to not touch it. I tapped it with my shoe and to my great surprise its wings popped out and it flew away. That bat was on my porch laying on my door mat. I am sure the bat would not have hurt me, but it would have given me quite a scare and it felt like something or someone was pranking me.

When my classes increased and I was making more money than I budgeted for, I decided to teach private classes, but it required me to buy a van. I purchased a forest-green van with three rows of seats. I was proud of my new purchase and knew it would pay for itself quickly and would help me move out of the mill house --that was my plan. I parked it in my driveway, left the motor running, and dashed in to get my checkbook to pay the Day Care when I picked up Mia. On my way back out to the van, a massive tree limb fell on the top of the van and the van was nearly a total loss. I tried to keep my composure and sense of humor, but this prank got the best of me. I had the van towed to one of the larger towns nearby. They said that they could have my van fixed by the following week and my insurance paid for everything including a rental car. I took the emotional blow and tried my best to move on.

After Mia turned a year and a half, I met the love of my life, Matthew. By grand appointment we were at the right place at the right time and connected. As Mama Jenny said nothing happens by coincidence so I counted my blessings.

The first day Mia saw Matthew, she said, "Daddy!" Matthew said, "No, darling, I am not your Daddy," and asked her to call him Daddy Matt, which she refused to do. It was like Mia and Matthew knew each other from times gone past. They loved the same food, shared the same movies, giggled, and played all the time, and the three of us held hands anywhere we walked that is unless Matthew was carrying Mia. Mia was crazy about Matthew. She climbed into his leather jacket with him in it and refused to get out. Any time someone had a bump, a scratch, or a broken item, Mia told them that her Daddy could fix it, "He can fix anything."

Matthew was quite the "fix it" man and what was most important is that he "fixed" my small little family as now with Matthew in our lives, it was no longer Mia and I against the world. Interestingly, when Mama Jenny met Matthew the first time, she turned to my mom and told her that he was going to be her son in law. It appeared that Mia and Mama Jenny recognized Matthew and I was never happier. Matthew and I got married and we were living happily, regardless to the strange paranormal activity, in our small mill home.

One night after I cooked dinner, I noticed that two of my figurines in my bedroom were missing. We scoured the house for them and could not find them. Matt went downstairs for some tools and he found the figurines on the pool table. We went out of town for a few days and thought we missed the paranormal prank but indeed we did not as when we returned home it happened. Sure enough, when the heater kicked on, we smelled rotten meat. We smelled the dinner I cooked, and it was fine. We ate dinner and got ready for bed thinking that maybe some smell outside that came through the air vents or windows. During the night that same rotten meat smell woke us up. I went into the bathroom and smelled it in there. Matt smelled in in the living room. As we were searching the house, it seemed like the smell would stop and start and also come from various directions. All of our moving around in the house woke Mia up. She sat up in the bed and was talking to her invisible friend. She suddenly yelled, "Wook Mama, An-gel!"

She was telling me she saw an angel. I had seen an angel as a child and mom could not see it and suddenly, I knew how mom felt. The pang in my heart for my mom was overwhelming. I did not have time for that right now because something was rotten in my home. Mia begged me to get her out of the bed and I told her to hang on Mommy was busy.

Matthew and I resorted to crawling around on the floor smelling for the scent of rotten meat. Finally, we got Mia out of the crib, put her in the bed with us and went back to sleep. Matt had enough that night and invited his best friend, James, to come to dinner the next day. I was so nervous James would judge me about the smell, but Matt explained what was going on and he joined the hunt. I prepared a snack for Mia, put it on her child sized table and chairs in the living room and turned on her princess movie while the three of us crawled around hunting the smell of rotten flesh. James and Matt ended up in the basement. I was holding my precious daughter when I heard one of the guys yelled to the other one that they found the foul smell. An opossum had fallen into my HVAC system and died on top of the heating unit. Every time the heat turned on it blew that rancid smell into our home. Matthew appeared with James, both wearing gas masks they had in their gear, with a huge bag wrapped in a tarp. I saw James and Matthew get in a truck with the tarped bag hanging out of the window, both men wearing gas masks, and they drove away. Mia turned to me and said, "My an-gel is Kelley with an E. Kelley with an E."

How in the world would my little girl know that Kelley could be spelled with an E? What an odd thing to say. Was the entity finally trying to speak to us? What kind of timing was this? What kind of life am I living? How does this type of thing happen in a home? Something is playing pranks on us and I think her name is Kelley with an E.

Mia was getting older and bigger. She was such a joy, totally fearless and into everything. She was trying to sleep in her crib converted to a child's bed but preferred to snuggle with mom and dad. We lowered her crib and she enjoyed the new height. She was nearly two-years old and we were trying to get more space in our bed. Mom showed up at the house with my old canopy bed. Mia was thrilled to have my princess bed and we were thrilled that she may sleep in her own bed. She slept in her bed for two nights in a row which was promising, and I braced myself for the next blow from Kelley with an E since it was perfect timing for a prank. The third night, Mia called me in her room shortly after she had dozed off to sleep as something woke her up. I went to her room to see what was going on, so I laid down in the bed with her to get her to go back to sleep. She heard something under her bed. Being determined to have her sleep in her bed, I stretched out in her bed and snuggled up with her, reassuring her that there were no monsters under her bed. Then, both of us heard something crunching under her bed. I stood up in the bed with Mia tucked under my arm like a football with her legs dangling behind me, and I screamed for Matthew. The whole time I was screaming, I was marching a high stepped march because I could not figure how to levitate. While Mia was screaming, "See I told you mama, I told you."

Matthew shot into Mia's bedroom and asked what was wrong. Clearly, we scared him badly. He started taking apart Mia's bed as if he were putting out a fire, to find the crunching sound underneath. He picked Mia and me up and put us on the dresser and returned to his mission of disassembly when he found a brown bag of candy under Mia's bed with her new kitten, Sassy, inside it. The mystery was solved, and we all headed to our bedroom to get some sleep as Mia sleeping in her disassembled bed was not happening. We all knew that kittens do not eat hard candy and realized that Kelley with an E had struck again.

Mia started K-4 as a three-year-old and was smarter than ever. Mia found all the pranks hilarious and she showed no signs of being scared. As Mia learned more words, she revealed more information. She wanted to wear dresses. Somehow my little toddler already had a fashion preference. She said Kelley wore a dress. Shortly after that paranormal statement, another bat flew into the house where Matthew made a contraption of mops, brooms, and bath towels to get it out of the home. Later, our television started turning on by itself and the answering service kicked in after the second ring despite our efforts to change the settings. The answering service gave us no time to answer the phone. I purchased a new TV remote and mom gave me a new answering service, but we knew the prank was coming. A large field rat was on the back porch which sounded like an elephant stomping through the jungle and Matthew handled that issue with ease, so we started laughing and wondering what was happening next.

One night, after I heard a small young girl's voice call for mom, I went into Mia's room and she was asleep. It happened again but this time it came from the kitchen. I knew I was in for the prank, so I got a glass of water and sat

110

in the rocking chair waiting for Kelley with an E to perform her worst practical joke. I heard footsteps up and down the efficiency apartment steps while Matthew and Mia were asleep. I wanted to handle this situation by myself as I was starting to get brave. I timed my actions toward the sound of the steps and opened the door abruptly to surprise the fiend on the stairs. To my surprise on the step landing was a huge black and grey tom cat that looked like it had been washed in the washing machine. His hair was tousled all over his body like cow licks, part of his ear was missing, and he had wildly, glowing, crazy eyes. He ran past me, climbed the wall like a ninja and dashed into my bathroom where he hid in the tub. Now, as luck would have it, I had to use the bathroom. Matthew was sound asleep, and I woke him up and told him the dilemma. He asked if I like cats, I said of course I do, and he said then I did not have a problem go to the bathroom. With great courage I went in my bathroom and sat down. I started hearing the demon cat in the tub making a sound I had never heard an animal make. I was sure he ascended from the pit of hell. Every time I made the smallest move, he acted like he was going to strike just like a snake. He meant to be the alpha and I may not live through this.

I kept saying, "Psttt... Matt! Pssst... Matt!" and he asked what in the world did I want in the middle of the night it was three in the morning.

Of course, he was asleep not knowing what was happening. I tried to turn the water on, and the cat jumped on the shower curtain, hanging by his claws; he glared at me. At great peril to my wellbeing, I finally screamed for Matt and he appeared at the bathroom door. At first, he was upset. Then he encountered the cat from hell and understood, because it hissed at him and again performed a ninja climb up the wall. Matt and I yelled, and we woke up Mia. She started screaming, "Don't hurt kitty, don't hurt kitty," as she ran to the bathroom. All three of us watched the wild demonic cat dive past our heads, fly across the kitchen bar and he took shelter in the kitchen cabinet. The fear factor from this feral cat showed us that we were not dealing with a normal animal.

Matt, wearing his boxer shorts, put on his boots, and my oven potholders. Fearing for his face, he took the wicker waste basket trash liner out of the basket and put the basket on his head. I was holding Mia and we were yelling for Matthew to be careful. He carefully and gently opened the kitchen cabinet and saw the bright eyes looking back at him. He reached in with the kitchen cabinet with potholders and secured the cat's head. Thank goodness Matthew had the basket on his head because that cat started fighting back and as his paws braced against the cabinet's threshold, the cat pushed canned tuna, flour, hot sauce, chocolate and a can of corn towards Matthew with such aim that it hit Matthew in the face so the basket was a smart idea. At that time, Matt backed up and changed strategy. All the experience Matthew got from the haunted prankster made Matt smarter and stronger. He got the barbeque tongs and tried it again stepping carefully through the wreckage of food on the kitchen floor. Matt struck first this time as he grabbed the cat's head with the tongs and yelled back at me to open the front door. Matt ran through the house with the cat in the tongs, he reached the front door, and pitched the tongs, cat, and kitchen potholders out of the house simultaneously on the lawn. We slammed the door and locked it. Matt pulled the basket off his head, thew it in the living room and said, "We are going to bed we can clean it up in the morning."

Close to 4:00 am, the Brown family finally found sleep. To our surprise it was short lived because mom and Mama Jenny rang the doorbell at 7:30 am to go yard sale shopping and dropped by unannounced as they often did. Personally, I think they felt that we needed back up. Immediately, after looking around at the battleground wreckage from the demonic cat, they asked if I was okay.

Mia rounded the corner of the kitchen and said, "Daddy threw a cat out on its head last night." Mama Jenny leaned over and quietly whispered, "Is everything really alright?" I told them about the newest adventure from Kelley with an E and the grandmas took Mia so that we could get some more sleep.

When the grandmas brought Mia back to the house, Mama Jenny and mom walked through the house using their spiritual abilities to sense whatever they could. Mia was bouncing on the bed and stopped when Mama Jenny walked up the foot of her canopy bed. Mama Jenny asked, "You have a beautiful little friend, don't you?"

Mia replied, "Kelley is an an-gel and it is Kelley with an E. She told me. She likes princess movies and likes mommy and daddy." Mama Jenny turned her head towards Matthew and me with a knowing look. She continued to walk around commenting to Mia about how much she likes her bedroom while Mia told her that Kelley likes her toy box and was like a fairy. Mia said, "Kelley told me I was a princess when I wear dresses."

Well, suddenly we understood why Mia always enjoyed wearing dresses. Also, Mia wore a Halloween costume of a fairy at home many nights so we found several more so we could rotate washing them. Mia's fairy costume suddenly rang a bell in our minds, and we realized that Kelley had been speaking with Mia often and they could see each other.

Mom asked Mia if she feared Kelley and Mia replied, "Oh, Nina that is silly."

I remembered that feeling when I saw the man in blue. More of these grandma mini spiritual walk throughs of our home were conducted over the time we lived in the small mill home. Each time the grandmas walked through; they discovered another piece of the paranormal puzzle, but we simply did not have all the information together yet.

When Mia was three years old, she was tall for her age. She was sleeping in my canopy bed she called the princess bed and enjoying playing in her room. She still saw Kelley with an E and the sting of the pranks had lessened I guess we were all starting to get used to each other. I got up to go to the bathroom in the middle of the night when I heard a little girl's laugh. Previously, I heard a young girl call mom, so this was different, and it sounded like Mia. I went to the bathroom and came back out to check on Mia. I heard a young girl's voice giggling again. It was Mia standing in her room with her back to me and she was laughing. I told her a second time to get in the bed. Even though Mia had gotten taller and her legs were getting longer, Mia looked taller than usual standing in her room. I pointed to the bed and that is when I saw Mia was asleep in her bed. Kelley put her hands up to her mouth and started giggling but I could not see her face as she was still keeping her back to me. I was half asleep, but I was wide awake now taking it all in, and I realized I was looking at Kelley. She was a good bit taller; she came at least to my waist. Everything I had happen in my life in the paranormal prepared me for this moment. I asked Kelley to come to me, she giggled louder. She scurried off quickly, went through my room, and down the steps to that efficiency apartment. I noticed that Mia recently started enjoying little prairie girl TV shows, and now I knew why, because Kelley looked very much like that without a bonnet. I sat on the end of Mia's bed looking down at my sleeping baby girl and I had confirmation she had seen Kelley all along. She was not afraid of her friend and I wanted to know what happened to the little girl that was a true prankster but still a child whose life had been cut short.

Matthew had finished the efficiency apartment, cut one of the trees down that had been dropping limbs, painted the hideous paneling in the kitchen, fixed the whoosh of the bathroom flush, and I had started several gardens in the yard. We were making the home something special although it had given us hell. It was time to start some major changes on our home and Matt planned on the tree project next. The tree project was much more than dealing with that tree as we uncovered information that we never expected.

When Matt cut the huge tree down, a limb knocked off a piece of the siding. That was when he got the biggest shock of his life from the small mill house. When the tree came down, it knocked loose some of the siding, so Matt took the siding away to fasten it again. He found multiple bullet holes in the back of the house hidden under the siding. He looked down and he saw bullet holes in the concrete sidewalk where they bounced. Then he found bullet holes in the wall that was the exterior to Mia's room and bullets were still in the house and he dug one of them out to show me. He noted that the bullet holes were .45 caliber which can pierce through homes and injure neighbors. Anyone would be alarmed if they found bullet holes in their home. What had happened here? Matthew started researching and calling local friends, one of his friends, a retired journalist, found out all the information that Matthew needed.

A week later, Matthew came into the house, yelled for me and I was in the efficiency apartment downstairs. I was sweeping and mopping when Matthew asked me to sit down for a moment. Mia was sweeping with her doll broom and continued to pretend playing house cleaning while Matthew and I talked. Propping the child sized broom against the wall, Mia had play dishes and was pretending to wash them in her play sink. Matthew told me that he had some information on the bullet holes in the house. I caught my breath as I knew that it would not be good news. Since Matthew purchased the home from the landlords, he had done all he could to help make the house a home for us. He had caught the landlord trying to add late fees and not applying the payments to the principle when we paid ahead to pay off the house. I knew when I signed the documents and I agreed to move in, they would be sly and underhanded. He fought long and hard for our home and now it seemed, we had more battles ahead.

He began slowly, "During the Great Depression, about 1934, Chiquola Mill had hundreds of workers participate in a national labor strike. The Chiquola Mill strike made the news all over the nation. The mill was making cloth just like the textile mills in our area where we grew up. The workers in Honea Path protested at the mill due to hazardous working conditions and low pay and large crowd of mill workers turned out. Child labor laws did not exist during this time and neither did safety regulations, so people were injured on a regular basis and paid little for their work. Children worked hard hours and were treated like adult laborers.

Due to the union organizing a protest, The Mill superintendent, Dan Beacham, who was also the Mayor of the town, instructed his maintenance men to mount a World War 1 era machine gun positioned on the top of that 4-story mill plus he had one hundred men with shot guns and pistols deputized adding to the twenty-six he already had as deputies. Although it is still unknown what caused the loud shouting and the fight that broke out, Dan Beacham was alarmed by the noise and authorized an open fire into the crowd of workers. Seven of the mill workers were killed and many more were wounded. The mill would not let the community have a funeral for the people that died so the families and friends had to dig their graves themselves. They also were expected to be back at work the next day even with injuries that people had gotten during the protest. The day of the shooting is called Bloody Thursday and it is surprising that the small town with a handful of red lights made the national news. The entire incident was covered up as the mill superintendent was also the Mayor. He said he was out of town and had witnesses to say he was not here, but everyone knew he was. Beacham's own grandson wrote a tell-all book about the incident much later. People will always be affected by the brutality knowing that these laborers died for the cause of everyone who participated.

My mind went back to my original thoughts about the spirit in the home having a dark secret. I also thought about the day I pulled up in the yard of the home and I wondered if the mill workers found close friendships as they did at the other mill village where I lived. Clearly, they were closely connect trying to survive the brutality, corruption, and conspiracy with their fellow employees. I burst into tears and Matthew held me. Mia came over and told me it would be OK. I felt horrible for the people of Chiquola Mill and their families.

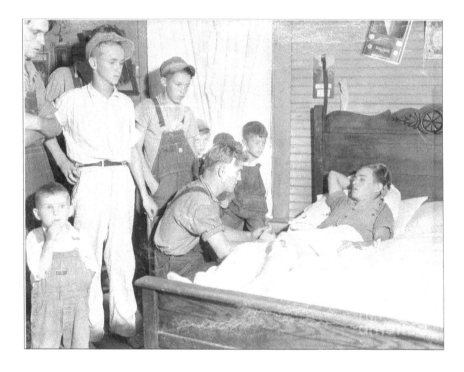

I was finished cleaning for the day, it was time to get quiet for the night. We went upstairs and I started setting the table for dinner. Mia was in the bathtub and Matt hung a towel on the rack for her. We ate our dinner and Mia went to bed. With the house quiet, Matthew and I sat in silence while we thought about Matthew's horrific discovery.

Matthew checked on Mia, then sat on the sofa beside me to give me more information. He said mill workers were brought into the mill village after they were injured. The actually brought them on our street since we were closest to the mill and our porch was used as triage. Who knows how many were injured during the hail of bullets and stampede of people trying to get away? Matthew knew a maintenance man in the Chiquola Mill many years later after the shooting, he disclosed to Matthew that the spent bullet shell casings were still on top of the mill and they had two other machine guns locked up on racks on top of the mill in the tower. No wonder the spirit in our home was trying to run off people. Matt said that there were thousands of mill workers that went on strike all over the United States to get more money and better working conditions. But this bloody strike raised national interest and made the national newspapers. There is a monument in the Dogwood Park not far from our home. Matthew felt we could go to the monument to pay our respects. If our home could speak, I wondered what it could tell us about what it had experienced the night of Bloody Thursday.

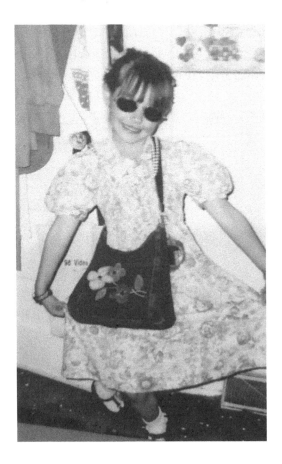

A little over a year later, I had my end of the year theater and dance performances. I used the puppets again as funding was cut so the puppets, even though everyone had seen them before, would still be used. I sewed the student's dance costumes in an effort to cut expenses. More economic cuts were made so I recycled everything I could for the performances. The middle schoolers were ready to entertain the primary and elementary school students and the parents. My dancers were ready in the prettiest costumes and everything was set. Mom helped me with my set up and presentation of photos.

I watched the 124 students I taught with a teary gleam in my eye. They did an amazing job and the burden of day to day was off my shoulders, so I reveled in the spotlight glow because I love watching children express themselves.

It was a bittersweet. Matthew, and I had decided, after years of sweat and tears, I would not renew my grant for the follow year. The stress of traveling, the constant changes to my classes and staff, and the lack of job security had gotten the best of me. I put in my two weeks' notice with the school and had obtained a job in a fortune 500 manufacturing facility. The benefits were amazing including their tuition reimbursement program, and the hours were perfect so that I could be home with Mia more.

Mia was excited that we would be moving closer to Nina and Mama Jenny so she was talking as fast as she could about playing with them and having fun. We started packing that same night and had family and friends helping us move.

As we moved, we thought about Kelley and what would happen to her. We found someone to rent our home and she was a nurse. We wondered how Kelley would treat the nurse but felt that peace was in the home and the nurse, being elderly and working in a nursing home, would be calm and soothing for Kelley. Shortly after we moved next door to Mama Jenny and Nina, Mia burst out of Mama Jenny's room and told all of that her angel Kelley with an E was in her house! She did not say goodbye! Over the years, as Mia grew, Mama Jenny, Nina, Matthew, and I saw Kelley even if it was just a second and we saw that Kelley was growing the same as Mia. They shared the same hair styles and same style of clothing and eventually Mia was as tall. Mia always called Kelley an angel and we agreed with her that Kelley wanted what was best for Mia. Even our new son, Elijah, saw Kelley and insisted she was an angel. Kelley was our angel and she was loved. The lesson we learned from Kelley was that anyone can be healed from a broken heart in any stage of life including the afterlife. I was honored to have been part of helping her mend her broken heart, but I am sure Mia did most of the work.

Around Christmas time, I was shopping for mom and Mama Jenny. Mia went with me to an antique store and insisted on wearing her dress and gloves. She walked by furniture and jewelry and she behaved like she was a grown lady admiring the merchandise. She was staying by my side until she saw a tea set. She asked me to read the price tag and I told her the tag read that it was a tea set from 1944 and price was $145. She had a smug look on her face and said that it was wrong that was not a tea set but a chocolate set. She said she knew because her daddy bought her one like it.

The owner of the antique store said, "My goodness I never saw a five-year-old that knew about antiques."

Mia said, "I don't know about antiques, I had one like that." So, the adventures with a psychic child never ends.

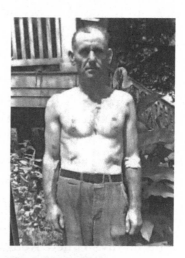

Chapter 11

Old Southern Hotel

One bitter cold winter's night, we bundled up, loaded out all our hand-held equipment, and packed extra batteries as where we were going, we would not have electricity. This was to be a quick investigation. We had finally gotten approval and clearance to investigate a historic hotel that had a ghost story legend attached to it so we were thrilled to get access.

The legend is that one day, a young girl in her twenties, with curly blonde hair, checked into the hotel. She asked for a room facing the railroad depot on the top floor. The young lady checked in with a little bag, went up to her room, and sat on the window seal looking at the train depot as if she were waiting for someone. When the train dropped off their passengers, witnesses claimed to watch her cry and shut the hotel window. The next day, her body was found hanging in the stairwell. Who was this woman and what caused her to kill herself? Hopefully, our investigation would give us the information we wanted.

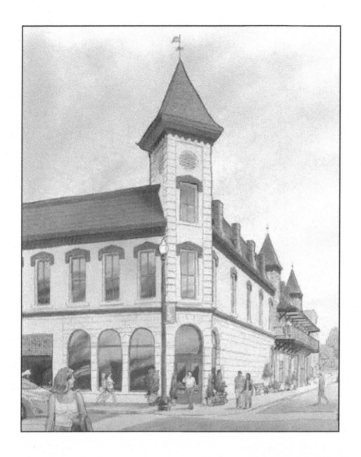

When we checked in with our guide/historian for the night, he/she gave us access to the hotel since it had been closed for many years she said that we couldn't go to the top floor as there was a gaping hole, a huge safety hazard. When I pressed her, she agreed to go with us to since she knew where the hazards were located. I was never so grateful for a brave lady who was more curious than frightened. She knew the legend well and wanted to know answers also. We walked on the cobblestone street to the hotel, she opened the creaking, antique door with a skeleton key. She turned the crystal doorknob and we walked into the lobby of the hotel. Truly we stepped back in time. I slowly approached the French gothic front desk and I visualized an older time when the hotel was at its peak, thriving, and bustling. To the left was a large staircase. Some of our team stayed in the lobby to investigate, and the others ascended the stairs to the mysterious girl's room. When we arrived at the top floor, we turned left into the landing and saw the hole in the floor. Carefully stepping around the hole, the historian made sure to check every step ensuring that we would not collapse with the floor if another rotten spot were nearby. We entered the ghostly room. It was exactly as the legend described. We could not open the window as it had been painted shut many years ago but we could see the view that the secretive woman saw, her last view while deciding to take her own life.

Matt finished situating the other teammates, ascended the stairs, and the historian and I met him at the dangerous cavity in the floor making sure he passed by it safely. We sprawled out in the floor in the room, on the ancient carpet, set out our equipment, and began asking questions to unseen ghostly spirits of the hotel. After being patient, asking gentle questions such as who would like to speak with us, what is your name, and other generic questions.

I asked, "Are you the woman that committed suicide?" I waited and I faintly psychically heard, "Yes."

My equipment did not pick it up so I continued to explain what my equipment was, how it works, and how she could register on it so that I could speak with her where others could hear her also. I returned to my questions and asked, "I have been so heartbroken that I felt like doing the same thing you did."

Matthew looked at me alarmed that I would admit something so personal and painful to an unseen spirit also in front of a historian of whom I just made acquaintance. I heard, "It wasn't that I wanted to end my life, you will never understand." Matthew and the historian heard it on the equipment but her words were somewhat hard to understand without my translation, so again, I explained how to use the equipment and also ensured the female spirit that nobody would judge her we simply wanted to know what happened to her.

With a clearly audible voice she indicated that her name was Hattie.

Matthew went back downstairs to get the other team members as we knew everyone wanted to see the equipment reactions to the conversation and we would need help communicating. When the team members arrived upstairs safely, they all sat down and turned on their equipment also, and we introduced ourselves to Hattie. I looked at the historian's face, clearly, she was moved when she heard

Hattie's voice, as youthful and innocent as it sounded. Hattie said she was in love and she did what she had to do. What a vague statement to make and I certainly did not understand what she meant. All our female investigators started discussing what questions would be next and strategized on how to coax Hattie to open up about her personal tragedy.

Terrie, one of our investigators, asked, "What happened to make you feel like you did not have any options but hang yourself?"

Terrie must have phrased her words perfectly because Hattie repeatedly said, "I didn't have a choice, I didn't have a choice, you don't understand, I didn't have a choice." As

Hattie's passions intensified, her voice got louder and louder. We had broken through Hattie's defensive wall and now we needed to ask more questions while Hattie was engaged. Hopefully, we could help Hattie in some way.

I said, "Hattie, the only way you will know if we understand is to tell us what happened to you. We are all women here except my husband who protects us and helps us, we want to know what happened. Is there something we can do to help you?"

Hattie said she did not have words to explain.

I asked her to touch me in hopes that I could sense her emotions and explain to the team. Hattie touched me on the back of my shoulder and instantly I saw something like a video of the past. As if I were Hattie, I was running with my small traveling case in my left hand, holding my hat on my head with my right. I just got off the train and was running to the hotel. I looked back over my shoulder over and over and felt my heart racing. I knew someone was pursuing Hattie and me, but I did not know who or why. I saw her hands sign the hotel registry; I watched her request the top corner room to keep an eye on the train depot and felt her head upstairs to the room. I watched her throw her bag down, kick off her shoes, open the window and stare at the train depot. I saw the sunset; the last train deposited their passengers and pulled away. With extreme sadness, Hattie and I paced the floor. I looked down through her eyes at her stomach and saw her rub her stomach repeatedly, cry hysterically, and dash out of the room. I wanted to scream for Hattie to stop but then she opened the janitor's closet and grabbed some type of cord that she found and then the vision stopped.

I became aware of my own surroundings as I stared down at the scuffed hardwood floors trying to clear my mind. Desiring to reconnect with Hattie, I knew I needed help so I explained in detail to everyone what I saw so that we could ask more questions. I knew there were clues in the vision, so we went over each step and then each investigator asked Hattie questions. We racked our brains for leading questions for Hattie. Matthew pointed out to us that she rubbed her stomach which made her more upset and that was a big clue. We all realized that she was pregnant.

One of our female investigators asked, "Oh my, if you were pregnant, is that why you chose to end your life?"

The response from Hattie was heartfelt and loving as she said, "No, I chose to protect us as there was no other way."

The historian pulled two of our investigators to the side, including Matthew, and started giving historic information. One listened while the other one was searching on her phone. The internet research based on the information the historian gave us, indicated that there was an embezzlement scandal on the railroad where the money for a large load of coal was "spent" but no coal was delivered. When the officials from the railroad verified the coal delivery, they did not find paperwork or inventory, so a formal inquiry started. As the heat turned up on the guilty party that embezzled the money, a railroad worker, an Asian man, walked into the office and inadvertently heard incriminating information on the embezzlement.

I turned to the paranormal equipment and asked Hattie, "Was the Asian railroad worker the father to your baby?"

She said gently and quietly, "Yes he is."

We all speculated as a group and concluded that Hattie was in love with the Asian railroad worker. He walked into the office at the wrong time and heard embezzlement secrets. When the guilty party saw him, he knew he spoke and understood English enough to repeat what he heard.

They chased the man and he disappeared heading to his beautiful blonde haired, blue eyed Hattie. He told her to run away, take the train to the town nearby, and he would meet her at the hotel and if he did not show up, she would know he was captured. When he did not show up, she knew the worst was realized for her lover as he most likely had been captured and murdered. If she gave birth to her baby, clearly the baby would have the appearance of its father and it would give her away that she probably also knew the secret of the embezzlement. What would happen to her baby if she and her lover were killed? Who would take care of the baby and love it? She knew it was not likely that she would survive, and the baby would endure hardship and abuse so her only alternative was to take her life and the life of her precious unborn child.

After we finished the speculation, our paranormal equipment lit up like Christmas lights blinking and flashing indicating that our theory was correct. We got our confirmation and also solved the mystery of why the beautiful Hattie committed suicide. The entire team was moved to tears and sadness.

She said, "Please do not be sad for me. They are all here."

All of us, stopped, waited, and listened for her next statement but we heard another voice. We heard a deeper voice with an accent. Could it be her Asian lover? He made it to the hotel in the afterlife.

"I am here," he said.

Then, we heard a baby crying. We heard them both calming the child and several of us asked at the same time, "Is the baby always a baby now?"

We heard a male voice say, "No, I grew up with my parents, I never knew or pain. I am with them and I know they love me."

Every one of us was moved to tears as we knew the baby's consciousness matured in the spirit realm and was often a baby for his mom and dad or sometimes, he manifested as a grown man. We found it so intriguing that the baby was able to cry like a child and then speak as an adult. He was an old soul and had special ability where he could mature himself as he grew in spirit. We realized that the ghostly family inhabited the hotel all these years loving each other even though they had suffered in life. So many people in the paranormal cross over spirits. We do not do that because most spirits are where they want to be, and their decisions are in their own timing. They beat the odds and were happy in their afterlife. None of us imagined that a spirit family could find each other and exist in such a manner. Their story will always remain in my heart as I realized that the healing could come at any point in life including the afterlife just as the case with Kelley with an E. Again, we were educated by what most people fear, and it blessed us. The ghostly family of the historic hotel touched our hearts.

I had an idea, so I asked, "Hattie, do you and your family ever leave the hotel? If you do, we investigated a restaurant on the other side of town that is haunted. Would you and your family like to make friends?" All of our lights on our equipment lit up and blinked and we felt their excitement as they had a new opportunity to make friends.

Together, the ghostly family said they wanted to meet the spirits of the restaurant so, luckily, the historian had the key to the upstairs storage of the historic restaurant. We spent some time introducing the spirits of the hotel to the spirits of the restaurant. What a novel idea to introduce spirt friends to each other. At this point, we felt like we simple had friends and the fact that they were in spirit was irrelevant. We heard laughter on our spirit box, and we knew they were enjoying themselves just as we were. Unfortunately, I could not see any of the spirits actually talking and meeting. That was fine with me because I could feel their excitement and I made a note on where I would be heading to visit, one of the many locations, when I become a spirit. I wonder if they are visiting each other now. Hey, it never hurts to make friends!

In this investigation we discovered that love truly conquerors all. The desire for the family to be together was stronger than life and death. They remain still today growing and learning in spirit while observing the changing times and changing environment around them. The hotel was recently renovated. What an exciting time for the spirits of the hotel as now they will have more guests to meet and learn from.

Final Notes

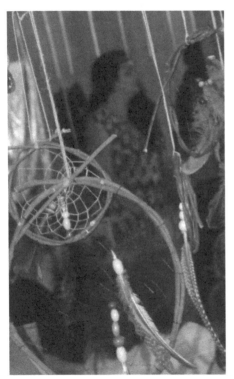

Photo Courtesy of Marjorie LaNelle

I speculated so many times in my life why my family dove into the supernatural. Once they had discovered they had spiritual gifts, they challenged themselves. There were so many aspects of their lives that were out of their control that they longed to command their spiritual gifts as a means to improve their lives. As luck would have it, the next generation of our family had spiritual gifts, and the next! Spiritual gifts can change everything about your awareness of the supernatural, of life after death and of spiritual gifts which gives you an advantage. I have big shoes to follow behind and I hope that I manage to at least not make them disappointed.

About The Author

Leitreanna Brown, a paranormal investigator, shaman, storyteller, and public speaker, is a native Southerner who is well acquainted with ghost stories of the South as her family worked with many of these cases. Her writing has appeared in Paranormal Underground Magazine, Fate Magazine, and Senior Magazine.

Leitreanna Terry-Brown, daughter of the late Allen Terry of the Ross Allen Serpentarium and Judy Terry, filmed her first television commercial for Romper Room at the age of 4 years old. She traveled with her father and many other famous celebrities which included the likes of Rick Flair, Elvis Presley, Crystal Gayle, The Bee Gees, and many, many others.

Photo Courtesy of James McInville

Her Paranormal Experience extends back to her family roots for generations where Leitreanna is 4th generation Ghost Hunter. Leitreanna, her husband Matthew Brown, and her children Mia Brown and Elijah Brown, have various degrees of psychic abilities. Her husband, Matthew Brown's specialty is analytical abilities and fierce technical experience. Matthew also lived in a very violently haunted home as a child and has had practical experience growing up dealing with spiritual activities that many people have never even seen.

Leitreanna is a registered Analytical Problem Solving Trainer, a Reiki Master, a Medical Qi Gong attunement 3, does crystal work, has studied chakra orientation, native American Folklore, and is a trained shaman. She is also approved by the church to conduct the rite of exorcism. She and her husband are Founders two paranormal groups. They are Founders of Paranormal Research Organization of the Southeast (PROS) where team members and family members participate in the investigations. They also founded Family Spirit which is an all family investigative team. The radio program that Leitreanna hosts shares the name, Family Spirit International, which has been running for twelve years and is currently on Dreagus Productions, JoshWho, 5 radio stations and also runs internationally.

Similar titles from Haunted Road Media:

THIS HOUSE, Amelia Cotter

Nora is a lonely fifteen-year old who dreams of more adventure than life in suburban Maryland can offer. Fascinated by the supernatural, she begins exploring an allegedly haunted abandoned house on the property where her father works. She soon finds herself tangled in the mysteries of the house as she uncovers its many secrets and meets a shy ghost called "Walter."

CIVIL WAR GHOSTS, Michelle Hamilton

While the War Between The States raged, the country's spirits were restless... Civil War Ghosts takes a look inside real ghost stories reported at the time of the Civil War and is a unique supernatural look at America while the states battled each other.

SOUL CONNECTION, Marla Brooks

When Rachel Warren went missing just two days before her wedding, her fiancé, Adam, was panic-stricken. 150 years later they were finally reunited but their joy was short-lived because they weren't the only ones from that last past life who managed to find their way back.

GHOSTS OF THE BLACK HAWK WAR, Dan Norvell

Paranormal investigators Dan Norvell and Larry Eissler take you inside a unique perspective of the Black Hawk War, a conflict between the United States and the Native American Sauk war chief, Black Hawk. Discover a time in Illinois's history rife with despair and tragedy that has produced a significant amount of paranormal activity.

Haunted Road Media

www.hauntedroadmedia.com

LEITREANNA BROWN

Made in USA - Kendallville, IN
27128_9781735668932
10.04.2022 1351